D1418058

Girls! Girls! Girls!

Girls! Girls! Girls!

Essays on Women and Music

Edited by Sarah Cooper

New York University Press
Washington Square, New York

First published in the U.S.A. in 1996 by
NEW YORK UNIVERSITY PRESS
Washington Square
New York, N.Y. 10003

First published in the UK by Cassell plc

Library of Congress Cataloging-in-Publication Data

Girls! Girls! Girls! : essays on women and music / edited by Sarah Cooper
p. cm.
Includes index.
ISBN 0–8147–1540–0 (cloth : alk. paper). — ISBN 0–8147–1541–9
(paper : alk. paper)
1. Women musicians. 2. Women composers. I. Cooper, Sarah.
ML82.G57 1996
780'.82—dc20 95–42778
CIP

contents

acknowledgements

I would like to thank my contributors for their patience in the face of my persistence.

Also Rosa and Liz for ideas, encouragement, compilation tapes and the opportunity to talk endlessly about music trivia.

And of course Catherine, I couldn't have done it without you.

introduction

'THIS IS NOT ANOTHER BOOK ABOUT WIMMIN IN ROCK.'[1]

For one thing its range is wider, extending from pop, rock and indie through to jazz, classical and opera, and also across cultures and geographical distance. I was not looking for evidence to reinforce the idea that there is some universal experience of music shared by all women. Instead this is a free-ranging diverse medley of ideas, impressions, truths, analysis and memory.

Your listening choice can have as much to say about you as the brand of jeans you wear. But we are talking here about more than just consumer choices. Music can also reveal cultural and class differences; the assumption being that the baroque music enthusiast will have little in common with the ragga girl. Music has always articulated important ethnic and national identities and aspirations, particularly for those excluded from the mainstream: Helen Kolawole refers in her piece to the description of rap as 'Black America's CNN'. But herein lie some of the seeds of music's contradictions. Black music in particular has long been identified with a struggle for equality, which is assumed – by a white liberal audience at least – to spill over into gender as well as race. But the rise and rise of gangsta rap has unsettled all this. In all the acres of press largely perpetrated by male commentators, an important perspective has been omitted: how do black women, often on the end of the rappers' 'appreciation', square their enjoyment of a music that is culturally resonant but can be so personally denigrating? Helen Kolawole effectively fills this gap by allowing young women fans to speak for themselves.

Pop and rock music have also been linked with ideas of rebellion, dissent and all-round alienation, from The Stooges to the Manic Street Preachers. But they can likewise carry, sometimes within the same song, essentially conservative notions of gender roles and sexuality. 'Indie', a term that now represents a musical style rather than label ownership, is often thought to be more liberal. But, in 'Velocity Girls', Laura Lee Davies destroys any illusions of this; and Liz Naylor echoes her arguments in her description of life as a press officer in the indie sector. And as for live performance, is it any surprise that most rock venues attract more men than women? Any glance at the 'Ladies' toilet facilities (or lack of them) and the venues' general ambience as younger, marginally hipper versions of working men's clubs, would tend to discourage all but the most determined woman.

Whatever the musical form, and from whatever culture it springs, where women appear, they are still the exception, and therefore the exotic, the other, 'the ultimate outsider',[2] surrounded by a web of generalizations and cliches. There is quite a lot of old tosh talked about women and music which I hope is refuted here: that women are emotional rather than cerebral, and generally nicer, softer and less aggressive, and that this is reflected in the music that they create or perform. There are flip sides to this of course: the temperamental diva, the mystic witch/singer, and the obsessive female fan. It is such images that allow women who appear clearly in control of their careers, such as Madonna, to be perceived as hard-nosed, manipulative and calculating, rather than having a balance of artistic integrity and good business sense that might be admired in someone like Elton John or The Artist Formerly Known As Prince.

Of course, strip down a stereotype and you will inevitably find an element of truth. The image of the record buyer or the concert goer or someone with an above average interest in music is that they are usually male, and this may be fairly accurate. But the problem with stereotypes is where they are used to support spurious notions that women have an intrinsic, genetic bias towards being singers, for example, rather than horn players, violinists rather than conductors, press officers rather than CEOs of record companies.

Somewhat disappointingly, the contributors here show that these assumptions cut across the genres. Even if many of their patrons see opera and classical music as transcending issues such as racism and sexism, Jennifer Barnes's and Sophie Fuller's pieces show them to be in the grip of conservative prejudices. In 'Dead White Men in Wigs', Sophie Fuller makes a cogent contribution to the rewriting of music's past to show just how significant the role was played by women. She also pin-points examples of current disadvantage: women conductors are few and far between, and despite an increasing number of women composers, only a minority of their work is recorded. Despite women music teachers outnumbering men, they are concentrated in schools rather than in higher education; and women remain incredibly unrepresented in classical music journalism and criticism.

In a world where success is increasingly viewed in commercial terms, and critics are less and less independent of the industry gravy train, arguments of artistic worth are readily sidelined in favour of the market. Women are seen as less likely to interest themselves in music in any systematic and acquisitive way.[3] This may be, as Caroline Sullivan argues (writing here about her experiences as a rock writer), because women are less prone to the train-spotter mentality of male music fans. Certainly everyone has enough personal and anecdotal evidence to back this up, but the reasons for this are more likely to be economic than essentialist. The crude fact remains: men, by and large, have more money.

If women do buy fewer CDs, their presumed sentimentality is seen to steer those purchases towards certain areas: pop, and 'lighter' (for which read slighter) classical and opera. In other words, work lacking the full artistic complexity of a Coltrane or a Wagner. But, despite this potentially unpromising image of the female consumer, the industry increasingly sees the promise of new and exploitable markets, and has developed strategies to target them. Most obviously, Warner have issued a series of classical compilations with themes – sometimes in a fairly tangential way – perceived as attractive to women: hence *Gardening Classics* and *Sensual Classics*. There is a pop/rock equivalent with the increasing success of 'love' compilations, where songs with overtly romantic themes are grouped together on an album whose cover usually features a sunset and a winsome-looking couple. In 1995 there were even issued a couple of classical compilations drawing on the strong homo-erotic tradition running through music, and aimed at what the industry probably considers a parallel market: gay men, as sentimental in taste, but with a bonus – more spending power.

The dismissal of pop as being for the girls, and not worthy of serious attention, tends to belie just how complex pop music has become in the 1990s. Even if much of it would not stand up to analysis in strictly musicological terms, at least it is not disingenuous enough to present itself as truth and beauty like the 'higher arts'. But this is hardly the point. A pop record, far from being simply the happy collision of a tune and a pretty face, is a conceit most likely to be delivered by a 'manufactured' group for whom – and for whose fans – the spin-off TV appearances, videos and clothing are as important as the music. In enjoying all this, the girls and young women, who largely make up a pop audience, are as sophisticated, not to say as cynical, as any of the postmodernist unstructured suits on the *Late Show*, even if their critical vocabulary may differ.

Pop music, in all its forms, has always assumed monumental significance during adolescence, as it soundtracks many of our rites of passage. Allegiances to particular groups and artists can take on almost tribal significance, and can help clarify identity in a swamp of sexual insecurity and fashion crises. Sometimes, though, we can make the wrong decision. Cath Carroll bravely confesses here to having been a Mud fan when she could have been a Bowie fan, and to having a mother who made her pass up Chelsea Girl in favour of British Home Stores. Rosa Ainley's sartorial mentors were not parents but hippy brothers, who did not understand the kudos imbued by a burgundy striped tank top. But, because or in spite of them, she rejected Nilsson and David Cassidy for Charlie Rich and Bobby Womack. Whilst both Cath and Rosa viewed their heroes from afar, Val Wilmer was lucky enough to meet one of hers: Margie Hendrix, lead singer of Ray Charles's backing group, The Raeletts. Her piece powerfully evokes both the excitement and embarrassment of meeting 'the first singer to set my soul on fire'.

In the West, Asian music generally has never had the exposure of African-derived musics. It would be hard to imagine popular music without the influence of the latter, but it is only in the mid 1990s that music such as bhangra has made any inroads in Britain. It has done so through hybrid forms of dance and ragga practised by such artists as Apache Indian and Bally Sagoo. But they are male, and in her piece 'Full of Eastern Promise', Sairah Awan puts Asian women very clearly on the musical map, as well as presenting a new way to view the experience of young Asian women in Britain.

Hispanic music also bears the imprint of migration in its development. In America it commands an enormous market, and one of its biggest stars is Gloria Estefan, who has successfully made the transition into pop. Sue Steward traces the story of her success and compares it to that of the long-standing Queen of Salsa, Celia Cruz. She sets their success against some of the obstacles women performers faced from a society founded on machismo, and the less celebratory stories of women like La Lupa.

When I originally envisaged this book, my impulse was to cast my net very wide, as I wanted to see what was there. When the pieces started to come in, I was fascinated by the disparate issues they raised, but I began to despair as to how I could ever link them all together. As well as coming from a range of cultural and musical perspectives, some contributors were writing as journalists, others as fans; some are academics, whilst others work in the industry. But as I put them together – bhangra with indie, swing with symphonies – a coherence gradually emerged. Even in the two most antipathetic musical forms here, there are analogies. The character and gender assassination that befalls women who feature in rap lyrics is not much improved on by what Jennifer Barnes shows to be the fate of mothers in opera – usually the death of a child or their own death. If women rappers find it hard to buck the music's sometimes relentless misogyny, they are as confined in this, in musical terms at least, as are the mothers in opera by their male composers or librettists. But the analogies are not all negative. In Lucy O'Brien's piece, a number of women musicians tell their own entertaining stories of life in a pre-pop world. Some are well-known, others are not. But what they all show is the strength and tenacity these women needed to survive, let alone sustain any sort of success. And that, if nothing else, is the point.

NOTES

1. Barney Hoskyns, 'Gang rap in the garden', *Observer Review*, 26 February 1995. This was one of two reviews of the admirable *The Sex Revolts*, Simon Reynolds and Joy Press, in which a male reviewer was anxious to set the book apart from the recent boom in writing about music from a female perspective.
2. Simon Reynolds and Joy Press, *The Sex Revolts: Gender, Rebellion and Rock 'n' Roll*, Serpent's Tail, London, 1995, p. 267.
3. Germaine Greer and Phil Sommerich, 'Why don't women buy CDs?', *BBC Music Magazine*, no. 34, September 1994.

sisters take the rap ... but talk back

1 sisters take the rap … but talk back

helen kolawole

'Who you calling a bitch?', asked Queen Latifah in her single U.N.I.T.Y. For many women rap fans the answer was all too obvious – the entire black female population. Of course there are exceptions to the rule – mainly the offending rappers' mothers, girlfriends and sisters – but any other woman with a sexual history is fair game for 'bitch-bashing'.

Latifah posed this question to all guilty rappers in light of the intense misogyny that has become increasingly prevalent in the rap world, and, in particular, in gangsta rap. When Aretha Franklin called for a little *Respect* almost three decades ago, she could not have predicted her plea would still be so relevant today. From the now infamous Wrecks'n'Effects *Rumpshaker* video, where women in swimwear shook their butts for all they were worth, to the censored groin close-ups in Snoop Doggy Dogg's *What's My Name?*, many female fans of rap have been left wondering exactly why they are listening to a music form that so often degrades women.

In the mid 1990s gangsta rap has become one of the most popular music forms amongst young people. Its enormous popularity transcends divisions of class, race and gender. But if the music has become synonymous with a profound misogyny, its artists can also boast a huge female following attracted by its energy and sexuality.

Gangsta rap is a distinct form of rap that originated from the West Coast of America. It draws much of its visual imagery from the blaxploitation movies of the 1970s such as *Shaft* and *Superfly*. The settings may have been updated for the 1990s, but the general stereotypes remain. Men feature as gun-toting misogynists who reinforce the sexual myths and associations of criminality that continue to plague black men to this day.

The image of the black woman has also seen little change. Women's role in rap is largely to appear as 'video hoes', placed on the screen for the titillation of the male audience. Very often the misogyny and violence become intermingled and indistinguishable.

In so much as gangsta rap is political, its main concern seems to be the plight of the black man. Gangsta rap is very successful at amplifying the nihilism felt by the black community, but fails to go much beyond that.

Ironically, when rap first appeared on the music scene, it was hailed, not only as an exciting new black music form, but as a vehicle for social comment. In very broad terms, rap continues to fulfil this role, but (at the risk of understatement) gangsta rap has never been concerned with political correctness.

In the early days of rap, groups such as Public Enemy complained of their lack of air-play on mainstream radio and on the music channel MTV. Public Enemy came from a style of rap which posed specific criticisms of American society. But gangsta rap, while it claims to document everyday existence as it is lived in the 'hood', is not so explicitly political. Rather, it places the aspirations of its protagonists within the consumerism and individualism imparted by its Southern California origins. Concerned with guns, drugs and women, rather than collective action or concepts of black community, gangsta rap has gained mass appeal as the music industry has been tripping over itself to accommodate the genre's new acts.

But gangsta rap has also become the focus of a rather different form of attention – moral panic. In the States, the war against the violence and misogyny of some gangsta rap has seen the alignment of some strange bedfellows. From former President George Bush to Jesse Jackson to President Clinton, it seems everyone has something to say on the subject. African-American academics and politicians have cited many reasons for the phenomenon. In the main, it is agreed that the problem lies with the deep sense of negativity that has engulfed the majority of African-American youth. However, there has been a backlash by the rappers, who have instinctively closed ranks and closed their ears to criticism. Some of them argue that anything which comes out from the ghetto is legitimate, simply because of its origins.

There is some support for this view within the black community. In particular, the criticism which rap attracts from women is seen by some as divisive within the broader context. Speaking to the American magazine *Vibe*, Ben Chavis – the former head of the National Association for the Advancement of Coloured People (NAACP) – expressed these sentiments: 'What I want to say is that I think it's retardant to the African-American struggle for freedom when sisters and brothers battle against each other. Our problem is not gender. Our problem is racism.'[1] Notwithstanding the latter, there are of course many black women who would challenge Mr Chavis's assertions. Black feminist writer bell hooks has noted the dilemma that gangsta rap further poses for black women. 'I'm drawn to the raw sexuality that is expressed in gangsta rap, even as I am turned off by the misogyny that surrounds that sexuality. How to get an articulation of a raw sexuality that is not misogynist is the unanswered space in rap.'[2]

For other black women, the issues are perhaps more spiritual. Delores Tucker, Chairwoman of the National Political Congress for Black Women (NPCBW), believes the misogyny and violence contained in rap is 'destroying the souls of our sisters'. Speaking at an anti-violence conference held in Washington in 1994, Ms Tucker denounced those rappers who indulged in the denigration of women, arguing, 'The continued dehumanization and negative depiction of women subjects our young people to offensive images that destroy their spirits.'

These are criticisms shared across some of the major divides in American society. Both concerned parents representing white middle America, where rap has gained enormous popularity, and parents raising children in deprived black communities, are worried about some of the messages being delivered on 'Black America's CNN'. Then there is Calvin Butt, the righteous reverend from Harlem on a mission to make rap purposeful again, although some have questioned the effectiveness of an attempted steamrollering of the offending articles in the middle of Harlem's main streets.

The solutions offered by the US government and the music industry have included attempts at outright censorship and the inclusion of parental advisory stickers on record sleeves. Similar tactics are used against white rock artists who have also offended mainstream moral values in their depictions of women and the use of allegedly satanic themes. But, as a way of controlling the content of both black and white music, these methods have more often than not backfired, guaranteeing heightened publicity and increased sales for the offending artist.

When many of the major record labels have come under severe criticism from activists for promoting misogyny, they have responded with some curious arguments. One of the most common justifications put forward by the music industry is the freedom of expression argument, something Americans hold dear as a constitutional right. Anti-misogyny campaigners have found this argument difficult to challenge. Jumping on the political correctness bandwagon (just at a time when the rest of America was jumping off it), the record labels claim to be providing an outlet for oppressed minorities to vent their anger. No such form of redress seems to exist for women.

Rap has consistently provided the music industry with some of the biggest-selling artists in the early to mid 1990s. But even its financial self-interest has been tempered by some artists pushing at the boundaries of liberalism. A notable, or rather notorious, example of this was provided in 1992 by FU2 on the flip side of their single *Booming in ya jeep*. At first the guys indulge in a little light S & M, such as safety pins through the woman's nipple, which is apparently nobody's business but their own. But the song goes on from what for many might be nothing more than an against the grain sexual fantasy, to a familiar world in rap that is apparently inhabited solely by the 'can't get enough fuck me 'til it hurts black bitch'.

The song was subsequently withdrawn by MCA after women workers complained to the company's executives. Could this be regarded as a victory for women who oppose misogyny? Sceptics would be correct in suspecting ulterior motives. The decision came at the same time as Warner Bros. were getting corporate cold feet over the furore surrounding Ice T's *Cop Killer* single. After protests from the police, from Warner Bros. shareholders, and from across the American political spectrum, the single was withdrawn, with the rapper's consent.

From a first glance at sales figures, it would appear that female rap fans have no quarrel with the intense 'bitch-bashing' that features in much of the lyrical content of gangsta rap. A great deal of the criticism vented seems to come from those with access to the media; not usually young black women. Rather we hear from indignant and enraged politicians or those seasoned in the delivery of sound-bites, not the fans themselves. Whilst the criticisms from those such as Dolores Tucker are of course valid, they are hardly from a generation of black women who could be described as fans of the genre.

It is inevitable then that female rap fans will look to female rap acts to give them a voice in redressing the balance. But how far is this viable? In the main, female rappers have gone no further than respond to what is produced by the men. This is not always for want of trying, but this reflects the position of all women in the music industry, unless they possess immense selling power.

Potential and established female rap acts face so many restrictions, never being allowed to cross the threshold into full-blown feminism, as their sexuality always remains their major selling point. There are exceptions to the rule, but, in the main, a female rapper must be seen as conventionally attractive, and maintain an accepted degree of sex appeal, in order to avoid being branded a man-hater or lesbian, or both. She may also find it easier not to attack her male contemporaries, for fear of being ostracized by the rap world. For black women artists who are already marginalized in the entertainment world, such ostracism may be too great a sacrifice.

Salt'n'Pepa have been the most successful female rap act both in Britain and the USA. The group has gone through several revamps since they first formed, but one factor has remained constant: a continual play on their sexuality. On the surface they portray the image of strong independent women who are in control, but the extent to which this is the reality is questionable. Near enough all groups, regardless of their musical direction, are subject to the dictates of the image makers. Today the group are extremely sexy; they may occasionally rap about 'no good men', but their liberation has not extended to being able to appear on stage without showing considerable amounts of cleavage or being clad in tight-fitting lycra. The image is strong, but it is still designed to be acceptable to men, even if men are not the main purchasers of their records.

Queen Latifah is one of the very few female rappers to respond in a constructive manner against the misogynists. Yet her stance is ambivalent, as she also owns a management company called the Flavor Unit, which has among its clients a rapper called Apache. Apache has in the past been known to indulge in a bit of 'bitch-bashing' himself, leaving Latifah fans a little perplexed about her commitment to ridding the rap world of misogyny. Despite this, Latifah's stance has led to rumours about her sexuality. She has on several occasions stated that she is heterosexual, but her 'unsexy image', along with her views, appear to be too much for the male-dominated world of rap to consume, with consequences for her sales.

Her 1994 single U.N.I.T.Y was a forthright attack on the 'bitch-bashing' that goes on both at street level and in the rap world. At one point in the track Latifah criticizes fellow female rapper YoYo for subscribing to the 'gangsta bitch' image. But Latifah suffers from the same problem as all her female contemporaries, whatever their image. They are simply not taken seriously, either by men or women.

YoYo is the self-proclaimed original 'gangsta bitch'. A protegée of Ice Cube, it might be ill considered to expect anything more enlightening from a woman who produces singles entitled *The Girl's got a Gun* or acts as a female pimp on *Macktress*. But once again it would appear that, like

Latifah, YoYo is grappling with her loyalties, as she has played a leading role in the formation of the Intelligent Black Women's Coalition.

The Lady of Rage is relatively new to the rap world and at the time of writing had not completed her first album. She is the first female rapper to be signed to the record label Deathrow, and her debut single *Afropuffs* did amazingly well for a female artist. Rage does not appear to be subscribing to the gangsta bitch image. She is forthright and sassy, but, in an interview with the music magazine *Touch*, was reluctant to come out against the misogyny of her fellow Deathrow artists. In fact she sought to justify it:

> I choose not to use those words. But people ask, how can I be around people who do. They're not talking about the respectable women who are out there doing their thing and trying to make it. They state plain and clear ... bitch, ho' ... you have those people out there. People who try to take what you have, or try to pin some kind of rape case on you for the money or media attention. I'm not a bitch, so I ain't never taken it personally. And they have never called me a bitch because I have never given them reason to.[3]

Being one of the boys seems to be a rudimentary requirement if a young woman wants to get her career started. Then even when she has made it, the world which she has penetrated remains so male-dominated that it is easier not to speak out. If the Lady of Rage gave a disappointing answer to a subject about which many female rap fans feel very strongly, now listen to the rapper Snoop Doggy Dogg's equally tired apologia given to a *Sunday Times* reporter. 'I don't diss women. I got a woman manager, my girlfriend and mother are women. I don't call them bitches. Bitches and hoes are girls who come up to me after the show and try to break me off when they don't even know me.'[4] If you did not know any better you might think that Snoop, whose lyrics point to a hard, blunt-smoking[5] brother who cares more about his mother than the 'hoes' and bitches who inhabit his records, had been coaching his fellow Deathrow colleague on how to give a standard reply to journalists who keep asking about misogyny.

So what do female rap fans make of it all? If a great many female fans have a broad sympathy for what can loosely be termed the women's movement, how do they reconcile their feminism with their love of music? The fact that the majority of these fans are young does not detract from the seriousness of the issues. All the young women I interviewed for this piece expressed dissatisfaction, to varying degrees, over the lyrical content of gangsta rap.

Marcia, seventeen, dedicated Snoop Doggy Dogg fan

'I went to his concert because I love Snoop's music. He's different, his sound is totally unique, you know, that Southern drawl of his is so appealing. Well I don't know how to put this any other way, it may sound strange, but I tend to ignore what he says about women. Sure, I think calling women bitches is out of order, but you just can't escape it. I think, if anything, I enjoy the music. You see, gangsta rap has a particular sound that is that much different to what's been around before. When I first heard Snoop rapping on a Dr Dre track, it was like a totally new experience. I think that gangsta rap is appealing because it is so raw, it's straight from the streets. In a way I suppose that excuses them using those words, because that's what they have been brought up with. But at the same time they could still make an effort to educate those younger boys, who do try and copy a lot of what they do and say. At the concert, when everyone was singing along with the bitch ho' lyrics, I didn't join in. I wouldn't describe myself as an out and out feminist, but I do believe in women's rights, so something inside me just wouldn't allow me to join in.

'I can't say that I'm a big fan of female rap. I like some of MC Lyte's stuff, and Boss, but there's not enough of them around. Salt'n'Pepa are really mainstream and I don't think people my age take them too seriously, but they do come across as being in control. These women have babies, hold down successful careers and look really good. When girls rap they sometimes diss men, and that's okay, but they are also positive in many respects. I think that men tend to concentrate too much on the negative and constantly get away with it, but I'm not sure how having more female rappers is going to change that. The change needs to come from the guys themselves.

'If I think about it too much then I would have to stop listening to gangsta rap, because it isn't saying anything positive to me. But it's hard because I do love the *music*. Do you understand what I'm saying – it's the *music* that appeals to me, not the lyrics. Any one girl in their right mind could not listen to a Snoop track and tell me, "Yeah, he's saying something really positive." You just have to ignore what's being said and concentrate on what makes you move.'

Some rappers, having become aware of the lack of positive vibes aimed at the *sistas*, have tried to redress the balance by turning their venom on white women. Amid the growing array of such tracks commending the beauty of black women is *Cave Bitch* from Ice Cube's 1993 album, *Lethal Injection*. In it he scathingly refers to 'stringy haired women' with figures like a 'six o'clock'.

Sweet T, twenty-three, lady DJ

'So he's gone from calling black women bitches to white women, so what? What's so radical about that? I must admit, when I first heard that tune, it did bring a smile to my face, because a lot of black women have a lot of anger about that. But when I think about it, I have played that track loads of times and I have seen black guys who date white girls nodding their head to it, and white girls dancing to it. How do you explain that? It's all crazy.

'A lot of girls have said this to me in the past, and asked, "How can you play this music?" Once, when I played *Cave Bitch* at a party, one girl came up to me and said, although she objected to inter-racial dating, that she thought that was the most degrading thing she had ever heard. I said, stick around, there's more where that came from. She was the sensitive type I guess, but she had a point.

'Believe me, I don't enjoy hearing guys rapping about sticking flashlights up women's vaginas, but my job is to play the music people want to hear, and that is what I do. I couldn't turn up at a party or a club and say, well this one and that one is not on my playlist for tonight. People would show me the door – a DJ has to play what is popular, and gangsta rap is popular at the moment.

'Personally, when I'm at home listening to music, I do "tut tut" at what is being said. I don't think the excuse that it is just a word is in the least bit acceptable, but I am in no position to do anything about it. It's like that ragga tune *Ride the Punanny*[6] by Bagaworries, the lyrics are absolutely disgusting. Once I danced to it in a club and I actually felt disgusted with myself afterwards. But what can you do? The tune is kicking, I love the tune, but the lyrics . . .

'You see, rap has progressed, or some might say regressed, from what it was in the 1980s. When rap first started up it had a happy vibe. It was all about partying and stuff. Then gradually there came the Afrocentric stuff – and that was really positive and conscious while it lasted – and now, now we have gangsta rap. Peace and loving your Nubian brothers and sisters is tired shit now, it's all about reality. Guns, wilding, smoking blunts, how many homies you've lost, how much time you've done, that kind of thing.

'Women get a raw deal because they are in no position to answer back, and because rap has always been dominated by men, no matter what form of rap it is. I guess a part of it is that black men feel that they don't have to follow what white men do. So they can go on calling women bitches and stuff, because they are a law unto themselves. Why do you think so many black people, women and men alike, still believe Tyson is innocent, or don't care if OJ Simpson really did kill his wife? It's all about media conspiracies, but they never want to look at their own dirty laundry.

'It's hard for lady DJs. There are not that many doors open to us, and to get booked it's like a real achievement. So I could never exercise my principles to a club owner or whatever – I think they would just look at me like I was crazy or something. Long live the rapper who comes out and says enough is enough; but let's be realistic, no one is going to change a format that is so successful. I think it's a shame that guys feel that dissing women makes them even more manly. I'd like to see what would happen to Snoop if he called his mother a bitch.'

Some women rappers advocate hitting back in the same way. *Mai Sista Izza Bitch* is the title of a single by the female rapper Boss who directly addresses the use of the word 'bitch', and urges women to get even and do the 'doggin'. But how constructive is such an approach. Is this just an eye for an eye? And how difficult is it for women rappers to get the chance to talk back, let alone put across an alternative message?

Yemi, twenty-six, aspiring rapper

'I see no reason why women should not be allowed to retaliate to the crap that is produced by some of the male artists although I understand why they are very rarely given the opportunity to do so. You should see some of the reactions we have had from the A&R men. From their limited perspective it's bad enough that we're women, but when they hear our lyrics they almost choke on their coffees. It's always the same reaction. "You're good but I think you could do well to tone it down a bit." We used to say, "What's the it y'all don't like?" We would make them spell it out in plain English. I mean, could you ever imagine someone saying to Ice T: "Yep, yep, I think you've got real talent, but could you just go a little easy on the misogyny, you know how sensitive these women can be."

'We have rapped about doing things to men's private parts, but it has always been tongue in cheek, though there is a serious message to it. Have you heard of Bitches With Attitude? Well they are not really a rap group, but I can guarantee, if enlightened women were running the music industry, they would never have even got past reception, let alone be given a contract.

'Rap is essentially a boys world. Its images are there for young adolescent boys. It's like rock – the women there are providing titillation for the men, and those female rock artists who break through still have to look pretty and not diss men too much. But just saying it's like rock does not excuse it – at the end of the day it is dangerous. It's telling young black men that they don't have to respect women. That they are nothing more than sex objects.

'As for all this "they ain't talking about me" bullshit – well I'm sorry, girlfriends, but it's reality time. I wish some of these young women could be flies on the wall when the men hang out. Maybe then they would realize that there is no distinction. For a lot of guys, "bitch" and "ho'" have become part of their vocabulary. They are words used to refer to women. It really is that simple.'

Josie, fifteen, waiting for inspiration

'Two Live Crew have got to be the worst for that, but I have never listened to them. I prefer the less hardcore stuff, or people who are saying something constructive. But if you go out, or you're in a friend's house and they're booming out the latest tune and it's saying something, then you're not going to appear lame and say "turn it off".

'My brother, who is fourteen, listens to all the gangsta rap tunes, and I hear him and his friends saying bitch this and bitch that. I just think they're immature, they are letting the music influence them. You know, some English boys act like they've just stepped off the plane from South Central LA or something.

'This is getting off the point a little, but I think it's relevant. When the film *Menace* II *Society* came out, I went to see it with some girlfriends, and we were amazed by the behaviour of the boys. Every time one of the characters said "bitch", it was like they loved it. I think they wanted to applaud. It's the same with rap. English boys know they can't go around calling girls bitches, because we will not stand for it. I can't understand how it's got to that stage in America.

'When I watch a rap video, and I see a whole load of girls dressed in bikinis, gyrating their hips around guys who have their faces in their crutches, I feel sick. It makes me angry, because I think I would like to be part of that scene.

What I mean is, I like the music, but I sure as hell ain't gonna go around calling myself no gangsta bitch, or letting any man call me that.

'I think that record companies should take a stand and not allow the rappers to say these things. Sometimes when I hear it, it makes me ashamed to be black even. White people must look at us and laugh, but their kids are listening to it as well, I suppose. My mum sometimes walks in when my brother is watching MTV and she can't believe what she sees. In some ways it's the generation gap, but it's also a woman thing.

'A lot of my friends at school idolize Snoop, I don't know why; but they think I'm a bit weird, because I don't check for him that much. I tell them it's what he says that I don't agree with, but I guess it's hard to go against what your friends are listening to. Nearly every black kid in Britain listens to rap. If it isn't rap then it's ragga, and that can be just as bad at times. I can't say that I have ever aired my opinions to the boys at school because they would just shout me down straight away, they think they're so bad, as if they live the lives of black kids in America.

'If I controlled a music label, I would make it a policy that all my acts had to respect women. And of course I would go out there and find all those good female acts that had never been given a chance because of the sexism in the industry. I'm sure if girls started rapping about how nasty men are, then there would be an uproar. They would probably say, two wrongs don't make a right. But it would be a real eye opener to see their reaction. You have lady rappers like Boss, but what does she sing? "You gotta let a ho' be a ho' ", and all that kind of thing. When I heard her last album, I thought she must be tripping or something, she was swearing more than the guys. The album was just full of bitch this and bitch that. Maybe she felt she had to outdo the guys or something.

'I like what I have heard from the Lady of Rage so far, but I'm disappointed by what she said in that interview. I think that deep down she knows it's wrong, but hey, Dr Dre signed her, didn't he, so what can she say? She's got to play the game. I am surprised though. When I heard *Afropuffs*, and she was talking about loosening up her bra straps, I thought, yeah – go there girl.'

There was a time, in rap's very early days, when a simple 'ho' consisted of something quite innocent – it was usually employed by a DJ to get a reaction from the crowd. He/she would shout 'ho', and the crowd would shout 'ho' back. But as the word took on a more lurid meaning, family acts such as MC Hammer were forced to drop these innocent rappisms, lest they be branded along with the rest.

The complacency of the music industry only serves to add weight to the argument that, just like the misogynist gangsta rappers, they don't give a fuck about producing positive role models for young black girls. If it sells in its millions, then that is justification enough for allowing artists to produce more and more of the same drivel. Female fans have little right of reply, apart from boycotting the records. But many of them do not want this because, as they say, they *love the music*.

As we have heard, the material produced by the female rappers cannot be relied upon to say anything more constructive than that of the men. Many of the female rappers appear to be in a quandary about the world in which they exist. Those behind the scenes will tell you that many of the female rappers actually do disapprove of the misogyny, but are tied by the constraints of the industry. For many female fans it seems ironic that, while the men are given a *carte blanche* to display every misogynist tendency they have, their female counterparts have to remain on the fence.

Some remain optimistic that things will change over time. Perhaps gangsta rap is just a musical phase that will peter out, only to be replaced by something else; but let us not forget that the 'bitch-bashing' has been around considerably longer than gangsta rap, and is not just the preserve of black music. Rock has an equally chequered past and present in this respect and to be fair to the rap world, not all hardcore acts employ misogyny in their lyrics, but – perversely and predictably enough – it is those who do who seem to gain the most attention, and for the present anyway, it is gangsta rap that predominates within the rap and even pop markets.

At least there is some resistance, but not all those involved are convinced of the benefits of outright censorship, nor can their differing agendas be reconciled. Meanwhile, female fans can only hope that more acts come along whose mainstay is not material derived totally from the sexual fantasies of adolescent boys. But they are not holding their breath.

NOTES

1. Kevin Powell, 'Soul on ice', *Vibe*, vol. 2, no. 9, November 1994.
2. bell hooks, *Outlaw Culture*, Routledge, London, 1994, p. 120.
3. Mia Mange, 'Interview with The Lady of Rage', *Touch*, vol. 2, no. 9, November 1994.
4. Caroline Sullivan, 'Cocking his leg at society', *Guardian*, 12 February 1994.
5. Smoking a joint.
6. Jamaican slang for vagina.

***d**ead **w**hite **m**en in **w**igs*

2 dead white men in wigs

women and classical music

sophie fuller

Many different kinds of music surround us in our fragmented late-twentieth-century lives, but there is one which the guardians of high culture privilege over all the others. It goes under many names, all of which define its superiority in one way or another: 'serious music', 'art music' or most commonly 'classical music'.

To enthusiasts, classical music is the supreme art form, conveying a world of powerful emotions from majesty or anger to fragile, ethereal, spine-tingling beauty. To others, classical music is the incomprehensible stuff heard on BBC Radio 3 or at concerts given by musicians in antiquated evening dress in an atmosphere of hushed attention and polite clapping. It is often seen as stuffy and boring, surrounded by an impenetrable mystique and dominated by the white middle- and upper-classes and – with a few glamorous exceptions – by men.

In a recent television programme, Errollyn Wallen, a black woman in her thirties, described the difficulty children often have in realizing and remembering that she is a composer, rather than a singer or an instrumentalist.[1] For them, and many others, the creator of classical music is a dead white man wearing a wig.

A complex and varied art form, classical music is in origin a Western genre, that has grown out of the music used for Christian worship and European folk traditions. Over the centuries it has travelled throughout the world, borrowing freely from other musics and cultures, although it remains dominated by a central Germanic canon from Bach through Beethoven to Brahms and Wagner.

Traditionally there are easily recognized boundaries between classical music and other music such as jazz, hip-hop, folk or rock. Large record shops have clearly defined classical departments, often carefully sound-proofed to keep out the tainted sounds of other genres. But in recent years the image of classical music has been changing. People working within the huge machinery of the classical musical industry – from individual performers and composers to promoters, broadcasters and recording executives – have realized that there are many ways in which classical music, both old and new, can attract a much wider and more diverse audience.

For an industry faced with dwindling and ageing audiences, a new approach has become a necessity. Composers, musicians and their music are being marketed in ways previously reserved for other products. Compilation CDs are sold to accompany an extraordinary range of activities, from driving and gardening to sexual foreplay. The friendly accessibility of Classic FM has challenged some of the elitist presumptions of Radio 3 (which has itself undergone a considerable facelift). Television has produced a number of user-friendly guides to opera, as well as BBC 2's trendy classical music magazine programme *The Score*. Luciano Pavarotti's performance of 'Nessun Dorma' from Puccini's *Turandot* was used as the theme tune for football's 1990 World Cup and opened millions of ears to opera.

Even contemporary classical music, often thought to be virtually unmarketable except to its few avid devotees, has reached dizzy heights. The London Sinfonietta's recording of Henryk Górecki's Third Symphony (1976) has sold over a million copies in the last two years while Michael Nyman's music for Jane Campion's film *The Piano* was short-listed for the 1994 Mercury Music Prize, rubbing shoulders with an album from teen idols Take That. Many of today's musicians and composers are eroding the boundaries between different kinds of music. The Brodsky String Quartet, who describe themselves as 'the garage band of classical music', have recorded an album with Elvis Costello; and the Smith String Quartet performed at The Ministry of Sound, while it was one of London's trendiest dance clubs. And in which department does a record shop now stock a composer such as Philip Glass or Laurie Anderson?

Classical music may be losing its elitist image and reaching out to become relevant and important to many more people. But what difference has this made to women's involvement? There is no doubt that women appear to be strangely absent from much of classical music's past. The canon of 'great music' and 'great musicians' that forms the core of classical music education or concert programming is almost exclusively male. Even in the 1990s, Macmillan's eight-volume series of books presenting the history of music 'in a broad context of socio-political, economic, intellectual and religious life' is entitled *Man and Music*.

But women have always played a far greater part in musical life than official histories might suggest. Much research has been done in recent years to re-examine the work of women throughout the classical music field. This research has rediscovered long forgotten and neglected performers, organizers and composers, as well as questioning some of the basic assumptions about what is of value in the musical past and present.[2] It has taken place alongside a growing body of feminist criticism which looks at how questions of power, gender, sexuality and the body are expressed through music, whether created or performed by women or men.[3] Of course, it is always important to remember that women's access to music making has varied enormously. Different times, places and societies have been more or less accepting of the contributions of different kinds of women. But whatever the obstacles they faced, women have been creating, performing and enabling music throughout history.

For centuries women were in a strangely paradoxical position as far as music was concerned. It was seen as a particularly 'feminine' art, and yet one in which women themselves were incapable of achieving the highest forms of expression. Learning to sing and play certain instruments, such as the harpsichord, piano, guitar or harp, was a vital part of a middle- or upper-class lady's training, providing her with accomplishments that were primarily important in enhancing her marriage prospects. But until the late nineteenth century these skills were only ever to be used in private, within the home. It is perhaps hard for us to realize the shame and disgrace that most middle- or upper-class women would have faced on appearing in a professional capacity on a public stage or even in print.

On the other hand, from the earliest days of medieval musical guilds, women from the working and artisan classes worked as professional musicians, especially if they came from musical families. There were, for example, highly successful women soloists working in Britain in the late eighteenth century. Primarily pianists, harpists and singers, several of these women also wrote and published their own music.

For a long time, however, women, from whatever class, were excluded from most of the education, networking and job opportunities through which male musicians and composers established successful careers. Although they were often at the centre of much amateur music-making, for most of classical music's past women were not allowed to play in professional orchestras, study music at universities or hold positions within the church (except occasionally as organists). Women were seen as physically incapable of playing instruments effectively and mentally incapable of actually writing music. Rev HR Haweis summed up the feelings of many in his popular book *Music and Morals*, first published in 1871 but being reprinted as late as 1912:

> **The woman's temperament is naturally artistic, not in a creative, but in a receptive, sense. A woman seldom writes good music, never great music: and, strange to say, many of the best singers have been incapable of giving even a good musical reading to the songs in which they have been most famous.[4]**

Widespread change in women's involvement in the musical world began in Britain towards the end of the nineteenth century, the age of the 'new woman' who was demanding and beginning to win access to a variety of careers and educational opportunities as well as the basic right to the vote and political representation. Slowly but surely, throughout the twentieth century, women have fought their way into the musical world, just as they have in many other fields that were previously dominated by men. In the 1990s women are to be found throughout the music industry. They are, of course, important consumers of classical music – attending concerts and buying recordings – although less frequently than men. Recent surveys have shown that a mere 36 per cent of HMV's classical customers are women, while only 42.4 per cent of the London Symphony Orchestra's audience for their concerts at London's Barbican Centre in 1992 were women.[5]

In the professional musical world of record companies, broadcasters, publishers, public sector arts administration, orchestras, choirs and other ensembles, women work in a variety of administrative and managerial jobs. Needless to say, as in most business or corporate organizations, women are rarely found at the top of the career ladder. Joanne Talbot has pointed out that, as of April 1994, 'None of the large self-governing orchestras has a woman in the top job – that is to say, the managing director.'[6]

Some jobs in the musical world, such as freelance PR consultancy or peripatetic instrumental teaching, are dominated by women. Such work tends not to be particularly well-paid or to have a clearly defined career structure. In music education most women are found teaching at school rather than university or college level, and here again they usually outnumber men.

University music departments and the fields of musicology and music analysis are notoriously conservative and resistant to change. It was not until 1921 that women were even allowed to receive music degrees from Oxford University (although the composer Elizabeth Stirling had passed the actual examination as early as 1856). Until very recently there have been exceptionally few women working as professors or heads of university music departments.[7]

This appears to be changing with recent appointments such as Rhian Samuel as head of the music department of Reading University, and Nicola LeFanu as Head of the Music Department and Professor of Music at York University. It is interesting that both Samuel and LeFanu are composers rather than musicologists or analysts. Male domination in the running of British conservatoires ended in 1993 with the appointment of Janet Ritterman as director of the Royal College of Music. One field in which women are surprisingly absent is that of music criticism and reviewing. A letter to *Classic* CD in 1993 pointed out that of the thirty-four contributors to one issue of that magazine there was not a single woman.[8]

In the musical world, most attention is paid to those in the public eye – performers, conductors and composers – however vital the contributions of those working behind the scenes. The number of women working as instrumentalists today is rapidly increasing. The Musicians Union, which represents approximately 30 per cent of musicians working in all areas of music, has kept records of its male and female members since 1962. In that year there were 30,189 paid-up members, of whom only 1,797 were women. At the end of 1993 there had not been a very large increase in the overall number of members (33,647) although far more of them (7,114) were women.

Over the years women have had to fight many battles in order to be accepted on to the concert platform as soloists, orchestral or chamber music players. Throughout the nineteenth century they were thought to be too physically weak to play many instruments, although individual soloists continued to make highly successful careers. But women performers were not only criticized for their vulnerable wombs or lack of strength. As recently as 1932, the British composer Kaikhosru Sorabji included a vitriolic chapter about women instrumentalists in his book *Around Music*:

> The musical intelligence of women instrumentalists shows almost invariably lack of grip and power. One is always conscious of a certain childishness, a naiveté of approach, an immaturity of mind, so that there is a feeling of strain produced in works calling for higher mental power, a sense as of someone struggling with a task beyond her strength.[9]

One of the hardest-fought battles was for women to be accepted into professional orchestras. In the late nineteenth century women reacted to their exclusion from the mainstream orchestras by forming their own all-women orchestras. These were both amateur and professional groups, and proved to be a vital training ground for many women musicians who were then able to take the place of the male musicians who had been called up to fight during the First World War. When the men returned, a fierce campaign to keep the women in the orchestras was waged by the Society of Women Musicians (formed in 1911) and by the indefatigable composer and feminist crusader Ethel Smyth.

An extraordinary range of arguments for excluding women was put forward by conductors, orchestral managers and committees. Thomas Beecham, who refused to have women players in his orchestra, is reputed to have said: 'The trouble with women in an orchestra is that if they are attractive it will upset my players and if they're not it will upset me.'[10]

When the Hallé orchestra under Hamilton Harty sacked all its women musicians in 1920, two reasons were given. The first was difficulty in finding suitable accommodation for women when the orchestra was on tour, and the second was that the women had been excluded for the sake of 'unity of style'. Ethel Smyth was typically scathing:

> Now will anyone bind a wet towel round his head (yes, *his* head, for only a man can expound the deeper workings of the male mind) and tell us what on earth this means? . . . You can talk of unity of style between static things, such as Italian violins, verses of a poem, houses in a street, bank clerks, priests, etc., but not in the case of a fluid force. Sex will not give it to 40 men of different talent, temperament, habit, digestions and schools; that is the conductor's office.[11]

Women continued to be excluded from many of the major British orchestras throughout the 1920s and 1930s – with the exception of the female harpist, described by Smyth as 'this solitary, daintily-clad, white-armed sample of womanhood among the black coats, as it might be a flower on a coal dump'.[12]

Several new all-women orchestras were formed, including the British Women's Symphony Orchestra and the London Women's Symphony Orchestra. It was not until after the Second World War that women began to be employed in orchestras in any significant numbers, and some orchestras remained all-male preserves for several decades. In 1970 conductor Zubin Mehta was able to proclaim 'I just don't think women should be in an orchestra.'[13] In 1979 conductor Herbert von Karajan made his infamous pronouncement: 'A woman's place is in the kitchen, not in the symphony orchestra.'[14]

There are no longer any orchestras in Britain that do not employ women, and the Docklands Sinfonietta even has its own creche facilities. But there are still areas of the orchestra, such as the brass or percussion sections, where women are rarely found. There is, for example, only one woman (Anne McAneney of the Orchestra of the Royal Ballet) who holds a Principal Trumpet chair in a major British orchestra.[15] Screened auditions are being increasingly used as a way of disguising the sex, race and age of the musician. There are still few black instrumentalists in the major orchestras. And although several soloists, such as viola player Jane Atkins, have achieved highly successful careers, a black musican will find that she is all too often assumed to work with soul or reggae rather than classical music.

The female singer has had a rather different history from that of other women musicians. Ingenious attempts have been made to avoid using women to provide high voices, from the still prevalent use of unbroken boys' voices to the rather extreme practice of castrating young boys to ensure that their voices would never break. The castrati were hugely popular as opera singers throughout the seventeenth and eighteenth centuries, until the rise of realism in opera, among other factors, led to the supremacy of the female diva.[16]

The female operatic diva, from Maria Malibran and Adelina Patti through to Maria Callas and Kathleen Battle, has found herself in the strange position of being worshipped as a goddess (the original meaning of the word 'diva'), while at the same time being regarded as capricious, demanding and difficult. This can be seen in the use of the title 'prima donna', originally simply a descriptive term, but now loaded with negative connotations. The complex history of the female singer is caught up in many of the issues surrounding women in general, such as a refusal to believe that a 'respectable' woman would appear on the public stage, or that a woman had any other than 'natural', unlearned talents.

In the later twentieth century, the sensational image of the diva has almost disappeared from the classical music world. Singers such as Jessye Norman or Kiri Te Kanawa have handed over the glamour, adulation and backstabbing to more popular stars such as Madonna. The contemporary British singer Lesley Garrett has a self-proclaimed mission to take opera 'to the people', and has cultivated a glamorous, sexy image that has in turn borrowed from Madonna herself.[17] Garrett's second CD was entitled

PriMaDonna and she caused an uproar by wearing a conical bra for her part in English National Opera's 1991 production of Strauss's *Die Fledermaus*.

Along with their male contemporaries, women soloists, whether singers or instrumentalists, are being marketed with all the hype and techniques of pop stars. But where men such as Nigel Kennedy sport tough, trendy haircuts and talk about football, women are more often still having to conform to the impracticable, over-dressed image of a bygone era. Glamour, as well as ability, are of vital importance in the careers of performers such as violinist Anne-Sofie Mutter, percussionist Evelyn Glennie or pianists Katia and Marielle Labeque. While sexiness is an important selling point, the portrayal of a performer as too sexy will almost inevitably bring into question not just her seriousness of purpose but even her ability.

Canadian cellist Ofra Harnoy caused a sensation with the cover and poster campaign for the second volume in her series of Vivaldi cello concertos which showed her lying on a chaise-longue in a low-cut dress, clutching her cello between her legs and staring moodily at the camera. After this image proved to detract from any discussion of her actual performance of the music, the tongue-in-cheek cover for the third volume of her series portrayed Harnoy in jeans and a white shirt, sitting upright on a sofa with her cello at a safe distance. Above her head is the cover of the old recording in a gilt frame.

The sexual connotations of the cello's playing position – legs wide astride – has made it an instrument that was for a long time regarded as particularly unsuitable for women. Some women were decorously playing the instrument 'side saddle' into the twentieth century, and as late as 1934 the BBC Symphony Orchestra had a ban on women cellists.[18]

What to wear on stage presents a problem for many women performers. The practical, power-dressing suits that so many business women discovered in the 1980s, and that are surely the equivalent of the male performer's ubiquitous lounge suit, are rarely seen on the concert platform. Baroque violinist Monica Huggett was driven to design herself a dress that she found comfortable to play in, only to find her next review compared it to a curtain. As she has complained: 'Is that relevant? If you're a man, you can appear night after night in your 15-year-old, ex-hire tail suit from Moss Bros. and nobody says a word.'[19] For recent publicity photographs, as featured on the cover of *Early Music Today*, Huggett wore a black leather jacket.[20] In the early years of the twentieth century, conductor Ethel Leginska (pseudonym of Ethel Liggins from Hull) attracted considerable attention when she threw out her evening dresses and developed her own version of male attire with plain black skirt, waistcoat and black velvet jacket. At the 1994 Proms performance of Ethel Smyth's opera *The Wreckers*, conductor Odaline de la Martinez appeared in a black suit complete with trousers and cummerbund.

The conductor of an orchestra, choir or chamber ensemble is in a position of very visible power – controlling the work of the other musicians and presenting their own interpretation of the composer's creation. It has been shown time and time again that many people (both men and women) have problems with women in such overt positions of power. American conductor JoAnn Falletta has talked about the difficulties women often have in making demands, and how she herself had to come to terms with her own socialization as supportive and gentle – qualities not often looked for or expected in a conductor.[21] There are still few women conductors, and conducting remains a very hard area for women to break into. Most women conductors in Britain today work primarily with groups they have formed themselves, from Wasfi Kani at Pimlico Opera and Anne Manson at Mecklenburgh Opera, to Martinez and her two ensembles – contemporary music group Lontano, and the European Women's Orchestra, an all-woman orchestra that specializes in playing repertoire by women composers.

A notable move into the mainstream has been made by Sian Edwards, recently appointed to the prestigious post of Musical Director at English National Opera. In August 1994 Manson became the first woman conductor to appear at the Salzburg festival, ironically at a performance where she conducted the Vienna Philharmonic, an orchestra which does not employ women instrumentalists.

The increasing visibility of the female conductor, as so often happens when women begin to challenge the male domination of any field, has provoked a backlash. In the 'Backstage' column of *Classical Music*, Robert Hartford produced an astounding condemnation which would have been quite extraordinary in 1894, let alone 1994:

> I have a problem with female conductors: their antics irritate me . . . . A woman can do the heavy stuff all right, aping masculine aggression. Let them do more of a man's work – pilot Concorde, fly to the moon, become Pope, run the country (steady on) but please, for the sake of my mental health, do not let them act out feminine wiles for the minor key passages. Stop them doing in public what is best done in the warm behind closed curtains or astride a Harley Davison. Prevent them, ye immortals, from tripping and flipping, preening and wheening, primping and crimping and swishing and

swashing their way through the dainty bits and putting their undulating bodies between me and the music.[22]

And so, finally, we come to what is usually regarded as the central role in the classical music machine – that of the composer. For centuries, women who wanted to express themselves creatively through writing music faced a wide range of obstacles, from lack of educational opportunities to the belief that women's brains were simply unable to cope with the complex abstract thought needed to create works such as symphonies or sonatas. In spite of the uphill struggle they faced, many remarkable women in Britain, such as Ann Mounsey Bartholomew, Maude Valérie White, Ethel Smyth or Rebecca Clarke, made successful careers as composers in the nineteenth and early twentieth centuries.

Just as women instrumentalists were expected to play with feminine delicacy, so women composers were expected to write in a simple, graceful style and to stick to genres such as songs or piano pieces. Not all women composers obliged. A reviewer of Smyth's Violin Sonata (1887) found it to be 'deficient in the feminine charm that might have been expected of a female composer'.[23] Along with several of her contemporaries, Smyth continually confounded critics with her powerful, large-scale works.[24]

The 1930s saw the early successes of a talented generation of women composers including Elisabeth Lutyens, Elizabeth Maconchy, Priaulx Rainier, Phyllis Tate and Grace Williams. These were women who were determined to be known as 'composers', not 'women composers', but nevertheless faced undoubted rejection and neglect from the British music establishment. During their lifetimes their music went in and out of fashion, although none of them ever stopped composing, and all produced, in their very different ways, richly inventive bodies of fascinating music that should form a vital part of twentieth-century British repertoire. But where now are the recordings, published scores or musicological studies of this music?

Are things better for the younger generations of women working as composers in Britain today? It seems that about 10 per cent of contemporary composers in Britain are women.[25] Is 10 per cent of the contemporary music heard at concerts by women composers? The 1994 Proms season included seventeen works by living British men and just one by a living British (although now expatriate) woman, Thea Musgrave. Other recent festivals demonstrated much more balanced programming. At the 1994 Cheltenham Festival there were nearly fifty performances of music by living British composers, of which eight were of music by women: three works by Judith Weir, four by Thea Musgrave and one by Ilona Sekacz. The 1994 Greenwich and Brighton festivals also saw many performances by a variety of women composers, while the 1994 Cardiff festival was 'a celebration of women in the arts', programmed by Odaline de la Martinez.[26]

Such figures are encouraging, although the overall number of women composers is disappointingly low. Many educationalists believe that, since composition has become a central and unavoidable part of the GCSE music examination, many more girls, having experience of creating their own music, will choose to continue to study composition at college or university.

There is no doubt that the recent changes in the classical music world have included an increased recognition that much of the work of women composers has been overlooked in the past, and a certain readiness to try and redress the balance and ensure that composers working today are given a hearing. Channel 4 recently broadcast a series of programmes about women in classical music and opera, which included a documentary about contemporary composers. Needless to say, this provoked a typical response from at least one reviewer: 'We had to endure an hour of the most painful, incoherent cacophony I've ever heard: the sounds of the pampered, self-pitying middle classes harping on at full whinge.'[27] One of the central points of the programme was that, although women composers are producing a variety of exciting work, they rarely have publishing contracts and few of their works are available as commercial recordings. If you had been excited by the Weir and Musgrave performances at the Cheltenham festival and wanted to explore other music by two of the best-known British women composers of today, you would have found very little in any record shop.[28] And where are the recordings of music by such highly regarded composers as Diana Burrell or Nicola LeFanu?

Perhaps because they have still not found a permanent place in the mainstream of musical life, many women find ways of side-stepping or ignoring the establishment. As with conductors, many women composers work with their own groups or within alternative networks. Janet Beat's group Soundstrata has given many performances of her electro-acoustic works, while Jane O'Leary's ensemble Concorde has become Ireland's leading contemporary music group. Nicola LeFanu's powerful opera *Blood Wedding* (1991–92) was commissioned by The Women's Playhouse Trust for a production that was directed, designed, written, composed and conducted entirely by women. The organization Women in Music (formed in 1987) has promoted many performances of women's music, and has recently embarked, in collaboration with the London Sinfonietta, on a competition to award a commission to an unpublished woman composer.

Some women find freedom from the establishment by working with electronic music, and producing all their own sounds in a studio, without having to rely on persuading performers to play their work. The pioneering electronic composer Daphne Oram has drawn a parallel with writers, pointing out that, historically, women novelists, who were able to work entirely on their own, have achieved considerable successes, while women dramatists, who have had to work within a patriarchal establishment, have had a much harder time.[29]

Perhaps a certain lack of acceptance by the establishment has led to women being particularly involved in breaking down some of the boundaries between different kinds of music. Enid Williams, formerly a member of the heavy metal band Girlschool, has moved into writing music theatre and opera. After a classical training at the Royal Academy of Music, Lindsay Cooper has worked in many different musical fields from experimental rock group Henry Cow through jazz, improvised and film music to works such as her *Concerto for Sopranino Saxophone and Strings*, commissioned by the European Women's Orchestra and first performed, with Cooper as soloist, in 1992.

Errollyn Wallen's output includes a wide range of music. Her concert repertoire includes three string quartets, the opera *Four Figures with Harlequin*, premiered by The Garden Venture of the Royal Opera House in 1993, and her stunning *Concerto for Percussion and Orchestra*, commissioned by the BBC for the Young Musician of the Year competition in 1994. She has also put together her own ad hoc group Ensemble X, which consists of musicians who, although classically trained, also have experience of playing other kinds of music. Ensemble X performs Wallen's own compositions such as *Having Gathered his Cohorts* (1991), a setting of three of her own poems for baritone and two clarinets, written 'in anger and despair' during the Gulf War. Another is *I Hate Waiting* (1991), also to her own text, for clarinet/voice, clarinet/sax/bass clarinet, piano/voice, acoustic/electric bass, trumpet, percussion, tape and live electronics. Wallen also writes songs in a popular, jazzy style which she performs in a trio of bass, drums and piano.

Composer Priti Paintal has her own group of musicians, Shiva Nova, which consists of musicians trained in the notated tradition of classical Western music as well as musicians trained in the improvisatory tradition of classical Indian music. The group, which plays music by both Paintal and other composers, is often joined by musicians from other improvising cultures such as jazz marimba player Orphy Robinson or kora player Tunde Jegede. Paintal's aim is 'to unite sound-worlds not cultures' and her own musical language has grown from the melodies, harmonies and rhythms of Indian classical and folk music, the rhythmic patterns of African music and the Western classical tradition.

A question often asked is whether women's music is different from that of men. There is no simple answer. Women composers working in Britain today are producing work of breath-taking diversity, and looking for common threads can be a thankless and pointless task. Yet within each individual's musical language it would surely be strange if the fact of her gender was not one of the many different aspects of herself to resonate in her chosen form of creativity. As Nicola LeFanu has asked, 'Could there be a music which did not reflect its maker?'[30]

In the field of texted music – songs, choral works and opera – women's choice of words has often produced works that are particularly expressive of women's experience. For example: Sally Beamish's *Magnificat* (1992) for two singers and ensemble; Jennifer Fowler's *Tell Out my Soul* (1980, revised 1984) for soprano, cello and piano; and Helen Roe's *And the Angel Departed from Her* (1986) for mezzo-soprano, flute, horn, marimba and string trio. These are all works by composers who are mothers and all express, in varying ways, emotions surrounding the birth of a child. Many operas by women have refreshingly powerful female characters, from Ethel Smyth's *The Boatswain's Mate* (1913–14), to Thea Musgrave's *Harriet, The Woman called Moses* (1985), or Nicola LeFanu's *Blood Wedding* (1991–92).

There is no doubt that women are playing an important and increasingly visible role in the classical musical world today, a world that is slowly growing more accepting of diversity, and beginning to leave behind some of its old prejudices and assumptions. But there is a long way to go. Women throughout the industry are only too rarely found in positions of influence and power. Women performers are still being judged on their looks before their actual performances, and women conductors are still a novelty. Works by women composers make up a mere fraction of contemporary music concerts, broadcasting, publishing or recording. But the determination of women should never be underestimated and classical music can only be the richer for including their many different voices.

NOTES

1. *To Mention But A Few*, Palindrome Productions' programme on women composers, broadcast on Channel 4, June 1994.
2. See, for example: Karin Pendle (ed.), *Women & Music: A History*, Indiana University Press, Bloomington and Indianapolis, 1991; Rhian Samuel and Julie Anne Sadie (eds.), *The New Grove Dictionary of Women Composers*, Macmillan, London, 1994; Sophie Fuller, *The Pandora Guide to Women Composers: Britain and the United States, 1629–present*, Pandora, London, 1994.
3. See, for example: Susan McClary, *Feminine Endings: Music, Gender, and Sexuality*, University of Minnesota Press, Minneapolis, 1991; Marcia Citron, *Gender and the Musical Canon*, Cambridge University Press, Cambridge, 1993; Ruth Solie (ed.), *Musicology and Difference: Gender and Sexuality in Music Scholarship*, University of California Press, Berkeley and Los Angeles, 1993; Susan Cook and Judy Tsou (eds.), *Cecilia Reclaimed: Feminist Perspectives on Gender and Music*, University of Illinois Press, Urbana and Chicago, 1994; Philip Brett, Elizabeth Wood and Gary Thomas (eds.), *Queering the Pitch: The New Gay and Lesbian Musicology*, Routledge, New York and London, 1994.
4. H R Haweis, *Music and Morals*, Longman, Green and Co., London, 1912, p. 110.
5. Germaine Greer and Phil Sommerich, 'Why don't women buy CDs?', *BBC Music Magazine*, September 1994, p. 36.
6. Joanne Talbot, 'Fair play', *Classical Music*, 16 April 1994, p. 24. This article on women in orchestral management is part of a series by Talbot on women in the classical music business. See also, 'Beyond the glass ceiling' (record and publishing companies), *Classical Music*, 23 October 1993; 'Close relations' (PR consultants and music marketing), *Classical Music*, 8 January 1994; 'A future in the balance' (academics and educationalists), *Classical Music*, 14 May 1994; 'Hidden Sounds' (composers), *Classical Music*, 23 October 1993; and 'Unsung Heroines' (composers), *Classical Music*, 5 March 1994.
7. In 1993 only 18 per cent of academics with permanent posts working in university music departments were women (see Talbot, 'A future in the balance', p. 20).
8. Letter from Ivan Dickens, *Classic CD*, April 1993, p. 17.
9. Kaikhosru Sorabji, *Around Music*, The Unicorn Press, London, 1932, p. 139.
10. Harold Atkins and Archie Newman, *Beecham Stories*, Robson Books, London, 1978, p. 70.
11. Ethel Smyth, *Streaks of Life*, Longman, Green and Co., London, 1921, p. 240.
12. Smyth, *Streaks of Life*, p. 239.

13. Quoted in Nick Kimberley, 'It's still an unsuitable job for a woman', *Independent on Sunday*, 11 April 1993, p. 20.
14. Quoted in Sally Morris and Kathie Prince, 'Calling the tune', *Spare Rib*, November 1986.
15. Andrew Stewart, 'Shiny and new', *Classical Music*, 5 March 1994, p. 17.
16. For a survey of the castrati and female divas through the ages, see Rupert Christiansen, *Prima Donna: A History*, Penguin Books, Harmondsworth, 1986.
17. See Alexander Waugh's interview with Garrett, 'A material girl', *CD Review*, November 1992, pp. 26–9.
18. Margaret Campbell, *The Great Cellists*, Victor Gollancz, London, 1988, Chapter XXV, 'Ladies on the bass line', pp. 200–9; and Ethel Smyth, *Female Pipings in Eden*, Peter Davies, London, 1934, p. 11.
19. Andrew Stewart, 'Gender blenders', *Classical Music*, 5 March 1994, p. 7.
20. *Early Music Today*, vol. 2, no. 2, March/April 1994.
21. J Michele Edwards, 'North America since 1920', in Karin Pendle (ed.), *Women & Music: A History*, Indiana University Press, Bloomington and Indianapolis, 1991.
22. Robert Hartford, *Classical Music*, 25 June 1994, p. 49.
23. Quoted in Christopher St John, *Ethel Smyth: A Biography*, Longman, Green and Co, London, 1959, p. 54.
24. For further discussion of the work of Victorian and Edwardian composers see my articles: 'Unearthing a world of music: Victorian and Edwardian women composers', *Women: A Cultural Review*; vol. 3, no. 1, Spring 1992, pp. 16–22; and 'British women song composers', in Brian Blyth Daubney (ed.), *Aspects of British Song*, British Music Society, 1992.
25. A statistic gathered from the *British Music Yearbook* 1994, Annabel Carter (ed.), Rhinegold Publishing, London, 1993, and the British Music Information Centre.
26. For further statistics see Nicola LeFanu, 'Master musician: an impregnable taboo?', *Contact*, no. 31, Autumn 1987, pp. 4–8.
27. Victor Lewis-Smith, 'Variations on a hard luck theme', *Evening Standard*, 20 June 1994, p. 57.
28. As of 1993 there was no CD available devoted entirely to Musgrave's music, although five works can be found on various compilation albums. Weir is slightly better represented with a Novello CD of three early dramatic works and seven other short pieces on compilation albums, including a work in the first volume of the ever-enterprising Odaline de la Martinez's series 'British Women Composers'.
29. Daphne Oram, 'Looking back . . . to see ahead', *Contemporary Music Review*, no. 11 ('Reclaiming the Muse'), 1994.
30. Nicola LeFanu, 'Master musician: an impregnable taboo?', p. 4

les gray's erection

3 les gray's erection

cath carroll

My first pop purchase was I *Didn't Know I Loved You (Til I Saw You Rock and Roll)* by Gary Glitter, and it was the echo on the vocal that did it, causing a nauseous thrill within, which seemed to come straight from Elvis. I would later get that same sense of queasiness listening to Radio Luxembourg but then it was the bad reception that caused me distress. There was something about the interference that gave the rather dreadful, Americanized evening radio shows a sense of mystery and distance, both physical and epochal. The echo gave the songs an unreachable quality as if they were coming from a different dimension, a peculiar combination of nostalgia and anticipation. It also happened when the noise of punk rock hit me. Somewhere in the middle, for some unknown reason, I was a Mud fan – but never a teenybopper. To be a teenybopper, you had to have people around you who felt the same way. Also you had to step outside your front door once in a while, beyond going to school.

Not very resourceful, I was in awe of the voracious spendthrift superfans who would write in to my lifeline, the weekly glossy *Music Star*. 'I have 2,356 Donnie pix plus 250 scarves and 6 hats. I must be his biggest fan. Please print this pic of me.' It would be a photo of a teenager posed in a bedroom next to a giant poster of a moon-faced Donny Osmond. She would have a feather cut, no eyebrows, and would be surrounded by a lot of shapeless soft toys, the sort that were called gonks. I had a few pictures on my wall, but since I had a great deal of difficulty getting a Saturday job (employers seemed to prefer people who were willing to speak), I could never afford to buy my way into this Page Three Gallery of Shame.

I had to adopt the Blue Peter approach to being a fan: a toilet roll, some sticky-backed plastic and a lot of imagination. And Wonderful Radio One. Tony Blackburn, DLT, Diddy David Hamilton and, in a rare manifestation of taste, my favourite, Johnny Walker. This was partly because he spoke in regular, cliche-free sentences, but also because of the heightened emotion associated with his reading out of the new Top Twenty each Tuesday lunchtime.

My first regular encounters with pop music happened when I had just turned eleven. The driver of the school bus listened to Radio One in the morning. It would be the hour when Tony Blackburn alternated playing the hits of today with the 'Revived 45s' of yesteryear. Roy Orbison's celestial agonies going head to head with the Temptations *Papa Was A Rolling Stone* ('Sensational!' crowed the unforgettable Uncle Tone).

It was a pretty decent initiation into pop music, marred only by Tone being obliged to play some stellar stinkers from the Radio One Playlist, such as *Blinded By the Light* by Manfred Mann's Earthband, which would send me into a rage, as would the similarly progressive whinging of Supertramp. They had the power to depress me more than a wet Monday in Bredbury,[1] and both were distinguished by their lack of that weird sexy echo. On the other hand, the dizzy resonance of those Glitterband records induced a kind of breathless expectation that made me want to stay out all night. (Actually, for me, staying out in Bredbury would have meant camping on the back lawn, a location noted for its shortage of both neon and the blue smoke of cigarettes.)

After Gary Glitter, I enjoyed a profound flirtation with Elton John as my hormones warmed up for the big one. I started inhaling Elt's record sleeves. It was a way of climbing into his world, I suppose, a little like listening for the sound of the sea in shells. That induced a strange nostalgic depression, bringing to mind old flyposters outside transport cafes, half-memories of being a small child. But most of all, what twisted my insides, and really made me think I was missing some big fun, was the smell of the solvent-impregnated cloth I used to clean my copy of *Honky Chateau*, and the printer's ink that lingered on the inside sleeve of *Don't Shoot Me, I'm Only The Piano Player*.

I eventually became a Mud fan. I was isolated. Two factors, initially independent of each other but ultimately reinforcing. My copy of *Mud Rock* and the two Elton John albums nestled cosily amongst my mother's vast collection of Joseph Locke (whose name I always thought was written Josy Flock) and Clancy Brothers discs. Now and again I'd make an attempt to get a little more progressive. Once someone lent me a copy of Deep Purple's *Machine Head*, promising that I would be 'amazed'. I stood by the music centre for three or four spins of *Maybe I'm a Leo*, waiting to get 'into' it. And I'm still waiting . . .

There is much of my history I would like to rewrite, and being a Mud fan when I could have been a Bowie fan is part of it. Certainly *John I'm Only Dancing* featured that echo, the sound of confused ecstasies. I was both hideously attracted to the dissolute noise and terrified by the alien sound which seemed entirely related to the fact that he was ONDRUGS. I saw him perform *John* on *Top Of The Pops* and was concerned. Men didn't look like that. What the hell was going on? The fact that I had spent a good deal of my conscious life, wishing that I – a biological female – was, one way or another, male, seemed entirely unrelated.

After all, I wasn't ONDRUGS and I could not figure out what it felt like, this drugs business. It seemed such an impenetrable notion, irreversible, cruel and somehow different. I thought it made the world sound strange, just as all that reverb and slapback gave me those funny feelings. I guessed drugs – whatever they were – gave you bad manners and impaired your modesty so that you didn't care who saw you naked.

The Rolling Stones – I hadn't realized they had a recording career. To me, they were just a bunch of girlie long-hairs, perpetually photographed walking down the steps of some courthouse or another because they'd been caught ONDRUGS again. They were somehow like an older version of all the local kids who would be at the bus stop when I got off the school bus. The ones who would bully and torture my rather splendid school uniform.

However, how to explain liking Mud? How about plain old bad taste? I must have accidentally overheard *Dyna-mite* just as the first rush of hormones that signalled the onset of adolescence hit me. A couple of the band affected 1950s-type garb: drainpipe pants, drape jackets and cool brothel creepers. I would have given up hockey to be a Teddy Boy.

Next thing I knew, an existence as a well-adjusted male with a number of jobs (including Batman, George Best and the dark-haired guy in *The Virginian*) started to fragment and I kept having this weird sensation of being a teenage frumpette in the 1970s, living in a ghastly northern town called Stockport. Fuck, no! Not Stockport and going to a school that had no boys in it.

The girl I had a crush on at school was the coolest. A thin, dirty blonde, she sometimes came to school looking like a laboratory rat that had been up all night, other times looking super androgo-gorgeous, with ferocious black liner smeared over her too wide-open eyes. Once a year we'd be allowed to wear our own clothes, as opposed to the very attractive school uniform. I hated this because I had to wear my purple British Home Stores slacks. Sally wore old denim over her Rod Stewart buttocks and austere thighs.

She said her boyfriend was a biker. (Twenty-four years old. With a moustache.) She was assured enough not to have to talk to the hateful trendy clique if she didn't want to. They'd talk to her anyway. She liked T. Rex and Bowie, and sometimes talked to me about Mud because she liked them too. The cliquey girls, who cradled their important breasts on folded arms as they walked, would never do that. I was, without a doubt, Miss Dweebosaurus DeLuxe. Look at the evidence: Mud, those purple BHS trews, the undisguised enthusiasm whilst playing hockey, liking the wrong Elton John tracks, making a cardboard copy of his Zoom glasses . . . and wearing them. Yet Sally still spoke to me. For sure, she rocked.

Now, whenever I hear the Black Crowes, I think of Sally; she's wearing her Rod Stewart tartan scarf, wafting into class late, her pale eyes pink-rimmed, her hair unwashed and yellow, looking (my god, is she ONDRUGS?) serenely bored. If the teachers called on her in class, she'd just stare at the book and say nothing. For some reason, they never made her explain herself.

Those teen years: the orange and white Selnec buses, the rain, the occasional journeys to Prestwich and Wilmslow to see occasional school-mates, Miner's make-up in mauve and sage green, the Mates range that came in palettes of brown and browner, and that awful frosted hospital-green eyelid stuff. It made me feel even less female, which was no longer the plan. I had to assimilate. Oh, and my bad sewing, the dreadful dress I'd made to approximate the one Nancy got at Chelsea Girl. (Mother: 'We're not buying anything from there. It's a two-bit dive. Come to British Home Stores.') My brown and beige acrylic tank top, the yellow puffy-sleeved blouse I made in school, the suffocating drab of Stockport market. Some rubbery pseudo-platform shoes from Saxone. They sagged in the middle as I walked, giving the impression of my loping on springs like the characters in *Scooby Doo*. An abandoned Space Hopper, slowly deflating in the garage. Being just-turned-thirteen.

I would go out rarely, for my friend at school lived several bus rides away and had her own extra-mural social life. Occasionally though, she would smuggle me into the weekly discos at her Jewish youth club. This would involve a great effort known as Hide the Shiksa, a scene of much intrigue. Julie would drape numerous stars of David about my person, stand back and wail, 'What are we going to do about that nose?' The vibe outside the door was mellow and all the girls smelled of shampoo. Then we went into something that felt like a hall of sonic mirrors. They were playing reggae,

Ken Boothe's *Everything I Own*. I had never been physically assaulted by sound before, and the too loud bass was confusing. It was like I lost sense of my physical boundaries. I felt joyously sick all night. Everybody got up to do that little dance to Sweet Sensation's *Sad Sweet Dreamer*. The room wobbled late into the evening. My ethnicity, incidentally, went unquestioned.

One wet night, I was allowed to venture to the other side of the county to go to Wilmslow Odeon with Nancy to see David Essex in *Stardust*. Nancy, designed for high heels and lipstick, was a fourteen-year-old testosterone magnet. The woozy theme song *Stardust* woofed through the cinema and my fillings buzzed. As Nancy was fighting off admirers, I was spiralling into that ondrugs world of echo, sex-without-love, glamorous rain and whatever else went on outside the Stockport area. Sonically, David Essex had the right idea, but the fact that he'd been in *Godspell* ruined it for me. Swinging Christians in brightly coloured clothes scared me more than an army of Mandraxed Marianne Faithfuls and Angie Bowies with their knickers down.

Around this time, the Bay City Rollers became notorious as the cause of teenage pandemonium. Every Tuesday afternoon, the Scottish group would record their TV show *Shang-A-Lang* at the Granada studios in Manchester. Afterwards, the Tartan Hordes who followed the Rollers would run amok in the streets. These superfans still wore feather cuts but had moved to half-mast trousers with a tartan stripe down the outer seam – the thin, white cotton ensuring that the panties of the wearer shone through the fabric in all their buttock-warping glory. These girls were alarming, but not as scary as the hefty Ziggy fans of previous years . . .

Now, they were tuff gurls. I don't really remember any aggro from males in the early 1970s. The people who would rough me up at bus stops were always butch-looking girls with orange-rinsed hedgehog haircuts who would say things like 'Are you looking at my boyfriend?' The great thing was, there were no boys anywhere to be seen when they said this. They all had 'Bowie' written in biro across the backs of their hands.

My first pop concert was Mud at the Apollo Theatre, Ardwick, some time in 1974. I must have gone on my own. I queued up the day the tickets went on sale and was somewhat suprised not to see the long lines of overnighters that I thought were compulsory at pop concerts. But what surprised me more was that they actually sold me a ticket. I was half expecting the Dweeb Police to quietly take me aside and explain that they couldn't possibly allow me to sit in the fourth row of Block A, knowing what they knew about me.

The most enduring memory of the night is the sickly feeling I got just thinking about being in the same building as Them just before They appeared on stage. The concert was too much to take in and it ran late. This was bad as my Dad was waiting for me outside. I couldn't leave until They announced it was over, for I was scared I would miss something. (What? The entire band shouting out their phone numbers? Giving away their trousers?) It was getting later and later and I was wishing they would go away SO BAD. Oh, high anxiety. If stomach acid were a usable fuel, our family could have powered the nation during those pesky 1970s power-cuts.

Mud were a curious lot. (I suppose we all were in the 1970s.) There was Rob Davis, the acutely girlish one who wore astounding dangly earrings and a breathless bouffant of golden curls. He really was pretty and *Music Star* assured us that he had a girlfriend and enjoyed entertaining the band with classical guitar-playing after their shows. That's right! Rob wasn't really like any of the other glam rockers who, as my dad noted, dressed like girls. The Sweet's Steve Priest (who I once impersonated to great effect in the school gym) always looked like a mechanic in lipstick to me. But Rob was different. Actually a little too different. I initially went for the sturdy and straight-looking Teddy Boy, Ray Stiles, who played bass. The drummer Dave Mount was out of the question as he pulled stupid faces on TOTP. Singer, Les Gray, looked a little too lank-haired and sleazy and he wore his cat-suits open to display his very 1970s pale, flat, furless chest. Ray, however, in addition to looking delightfully retro, had an exciting V of chest fur lurking in his open-neck shirt. But then Gray played his ace: he began to sing like Elvis for their song *Tiger Feet*. Someone had turned up the reverb. Say hello to me, the future Mrs Les Gray.

I am thinking of a magazine pin-up photo of Mud, lined in a sub song'n'dance pose. They were wearing those sky-blue cat-suits. My class-mate Julie wordlessly pointed to something that I already noticed; Les Gray had a little erection going. I definitely felt let down. This disappointment had nothing to do with Mr Gray's, er, dimensions, or even this public display of the fruits of Eros. It was his oblivious and delirious grin. Why wasn't his face fractured and twisted by passion? Shortly after I had a dream that I was a man – not Les Gray, but certainly someone other than me, which was good enough. In this dream I had an ardent hard-on. Although I wasn't sure what to expect from an erection, I couldn't unzip my pants fast enough to find out. Whereupon the dream mutated and I awoke. I am still very disappointed.

I went to see Mud again in 1975 at Stockport's Davenport Theatre with *la belle* Nancy. After the house lights came on, we were about to leave when we saw that Ray Stiles himself had come to the front to sign autographs. I was stunned. I was even more stunned to find that I didn't have a pen for him to use. But Ray did. Bless his furry little shirt-V. The drummer, Dave Mount, appeared briefly at the back, only to wave an imperious 'no' to an autograph request. Well, sod you, Mr Mount. The last time I looked you were just the bloody drummer.

We milled half-heartedly by the stage door. The security man, who looked to be all of seventeen years old, sheepishly turned down the offer of untold sexual delights made to him by a fat twelve-year-old. (Not me. Hey!) It was all a bit of a strain, dealing with Them being there in reality and feeling obliged to get as close to them as possible, so we were all relieved when we heard that Mud Had Left The Building.

When my passion for Mud waned and my self-abuse skills improved, I'd end up listening at night to Fab 208 – Radio Luxembourg – because Radio One was off the air, except for John Peel who played awful weirdie-beardie prog. rock. I would usually be in the bathroom at this time of night. Fab 208 would come whistling through the stratosphere to be clumsily intercepted by our prehistoric transistor. It was a strange new un-Radio One-ish world; no DLT or Jimmy Young. It harboured Kid Jensen and some other guys who looked like girls. After every other song, they would run an advert for Alberto Balsam VO5 apple shampoo. For some reason this always came through the ether perfectly clearly. I cannot look at an apple now without hearing the vigorous chorus of 'Shiny, shiny, shiny as an apple'. Scarred, that's what I am.

Advertising on the radio struck me as a very decadent thing (commercial radio in the shape of Picadilly 261 had yet to appear in Manchester) for I was raised by the BBC and brand names were just not nice. But the Clearasil ad made me feel somehow wistful. Fab 208 did have one thing in its favour, which was a more liberal playlist than the Beeb. They would play Donna Summer's *Love To Love You* and I'd get that sick feeling, hearing her moaning through sibilant space, between signal breakup and the inevitable blurting of some Russian broadcast.

Did I mention that another of my aims was to actually be in Mud? I had to keep that quiet in case Rob Davis found out, for I wanted to be the guitarist. That ambition died after I spent the next summer holidays locked in my bedroom, listening to the US Top Forty. By now I was truly tired of garage mechanics from Sidcup dressed in lime green jump-suits. I had discovered the new Four Seasons.

It was their drummer, Gerry Polci. He sang like a girl and looked like a man. I completely lost interest in England until punk rescued me two years later. Now my nights were spent playing air wah-wah guitar in my room; wakka-chukka, whakka-chukka. I went to see them play and noted that Frankie Valli was actually about the same size as I was. Maybe I could wear his clothes . . . maybe I could have his job. Maybe I'd get to shag the drummer. I was perfecting my part on *Swearin' To God* when my dad yelled something up the stairs. Elvis has died. Suddenly, I didn't want to do too much of anything any more.

NOTES

1. Sub-division of Stockport. Where we lived. To be avoided.

worlds apart?

4 worlds apart?

salsa queen to pops princess

sue steward

New York 1981: backstage at Madison Square Gardens. A group of people had begun to gather below the steps leading to the stage, as a short, stocky, heavily made-up woman with a high, beehive hairdo was being helped into a pair of impossibly constructed shoes with no apparent heel. She had a towel draped around her shoulders like a prize fight boxer; someone removed it to reveal a dazzling, floor-length, spangled sheath dress. The woman looked behind at us and threw an enormous smile, then she strode up the steps and on to the stage. At that moment, a noise ricocheted around the auditorium: a cross between Concorde, a football crowd and a Beatles audience circa 1965. The band broke into the opening bars of a song and there was a break in the tumult as a flurry of long, deep, growled notes rushed through the air. There was a mighty roar as she tore into a song which rocked and shook the entire building . . . Welcome to the Celia Cruz experience.

Celia sang for over an hour, a programme which satisfied everyone in the house: irresistibly quaint old Cuban songs, drenched with the nostalgia of exile, and refurbished hits from her 1950s repertoire with the orchestra La Sonora Matancera, both recalling her days as the toast of Havana. She also gave us raw, uptempo, modern salsa, crafted in New York's Fania Records factory, songs which launched the second stage of her career, in the USA and on to the wider sphere of 'World Music'. She sang praises to the Fania All-Stars orchestra playing behind her; the percussionists taunted her with their rhythms and she ad-libbed and traded rhymes with the chorus of Fania males who crooned their responses with obvious enchantment. And she danced, she skipped and skittered and sashayed, gliding around the stage like a young girl, performing for audience and orchestra alike, but also, very definitely, for herself. The audience were frenzied the whole time, calling to her, waving their arms towards her, singing every chorus with her. She talked to them confidentially, boasting about her extraordinary sparkly dress, updating them on her musician friends and her husband Pedro – who stood tall and silent at the side of the gigantic stage, minutely absorbing every detail of every song. In the protracted *Bemba Colora*, her signature tune finale, and an extravagant vehicle for her improvisational skills, she offered the audience their chance to express themselves, asking rhetorically, 'What's my name?' They roared, 'Celia Cruz.'

I've lost count of the times I have witnessed Celia Cruz perform since that memorable night, but I've never seen her disappoint an audience. There were nights when her feet were swollen from exhaustion (and those shoes!), and I watched Tito Puente massage them before she glided back on stage. Sometimes the exhaustion of travelling the world for anything up to nine months of each year – and the very occasional reminder that she was in her sixth, or maybe seventh, decade – meant she was so tired she could barely speak. But as she stepped on any stage, these factors evaporated instantly – and the star burst forth to fill the room.

Celia Cruz's powers of communication are phenomenal. I remember seeing this tested on a summer's night in 1993. In Manchester for the first time, she performed with Tito Puente's orchestra in a community centre in the outskirts of town, to people who had, initially, no idea what she was singing about, and no comprehension of the meaning and nuances of salsa. She had to work extra hard to banish the cultural differences in an audience more attuned to rock and jazz, and she achieved it partly by appealing to each person individually, regardless of the language barrier. Within a short time, the whole hall had been captivated by the sheer power and range of her voice. Like all great artists, Celia Cruz cuts through to a spiritual level beyond exact words.

Within Latin America, Celia Cruz possesses an almost divine status. She has captured the collective imagination of each new generation for almost half a century. She is universally known as 'The Queen of Salsa', and feted like royalty. She jokes about possessing the keys of every city in the Latin world – and that includes Miami, New York, and Los Angeles. Her records sell in vast numbers, from her earliest collections of songs from the 1950s in Havana, to the latest salsa-rap experiments with the producer Willie Colon. And she shows no sign of retiring.

At first glance, there is maybe something incongruous about a woman rising above the myriad male singers in salsa, to occupy this select slot. Latin American society is seldom known for its tolerance of striving women, and, in order to achieve her position, Celia Cruz had to compete with scores of male *salseros* throughout her early years.

Her success derives partly from her enormous determination and talent, but it also reveals some interesting contradictions in Latin American society. Before looking at this in any detail, I cannot resist making comparisons between Celia Cruz and women in other musical cultures (though caution is needed when making any such analogies). The Egyptian singer, Oum Kalthoum, who died in 1975, had 'reigned supreme' throughout the Arab world for about forty years. Like Celia, Kalthoum achieved near divine status in a society where women's lives and destinies were (and often still are) thoroughly circumscribed from birth.

Born in 1910, Oum Kalthoum began to sing, in the 1920s, religious texts and classical love poetry taught by her father, an imam. It is said that he would dress her as a boy to get her into religious gatherings. She was 'talent spotted' by two visiting musicians from Cairo who invited her there to study classical Arabic music. Her reputation grew and she made her first record in 1924; within a decade, she was the top artiste on Cairo radio, and a legend throughout Egypt.

Oum's appeal was her exceptional skill at improvisation, which is central to classic Arab song. She boasted that she never sang even a verse the same way twice, and could spin out a song – especially a love song – for up to an hour, keeping her audiences entranced, and driving them to heights of ecstasy like a religious orator. Her fame spread beyond Egypt, to the point where she symbolically unified the whole Arab world. Cairo Radio gave her a weekly live show, which literally brought the country to a halt. When President Sadat once unwisely tried to broadcast to the nation during her time slot, nobody listened. At her funeral in February 1975, three million people followed her coffin through the streets of Cairo, and heads of state from all around the Arab world attended. Even today, she is celebrated on Egyptian radio with a monthly concert hour.

Physically, Oum Kalthoum was not a conventional beauty: she performed standing still, wearing heavy dark-rimmed glasses, long traditional robes, and moved only one arm to wave a long white scarf (rumoured to be drenched in opium juice). She ignored the tradition of belly dancing which so many singers use to accompany their songs; her popularity was based entirely on her singing.

There are many tempting comparisons to be made between Celia Cruz and Oum Kalthoum. Both inhabited overtly male-dominated societies where religion still actively governs women's lifestyles and destinies, and traditional family values prevail. Both women entered these rigid men's worlds and retained control of their own identity and professional destiny – and survived for many decades, travelling like empresses throughout their extended territories.

Popular music from all around the world is full of similar examples of women who achieve such exalted positions. They are familiar in the rock and pop worlds; but in cultures famous for their intense restrictions on women's lives, they seem like strange anomalies, inspirational exceptions. It is also obvious that in most cases, only one such woman at a time enjoys that status. While it is perhaps simplistic to suggest that there can only be one madonna, one mother, these are, after all, respected roles; and away from the reach of state control, women do exert a surprising amount of power within the strong family structures that exist. In politics, too, women occasionally play leading roles: Israel's Golda Meir, Pakistan's Benazir Bhutto, the Phillipines' Cory Aquino, and, of course, Indira Ghandi. This is more often than not the result of dynastic processes, through a father or husband. But many of these same cultures have given rise to an Oum Kalthoum or a Celia Cruz who occupies the apex of the entertainment business.

India's massive and enormously prolific film industry has always relied on the skills of so-called 'playback' singers, who sing all the soundtracks. For nearly half a century, Asha Bohsle and her now retired sister, Lata Mangeshkar, have between them recorded countless thousands of songs (an estimated 25,000) and are respected throughout the sub-continent as elder stateswomen. Like Oum Kalthoum, the songs of these two middle-aged Indian women have united the people of the physically and politically divided sub-continent for over half a century.

But for every one of these women to succeed and stay at the top, there are scores of less fortunate female performers who have never got through, or who were rapidly drained of the status they once possessed (invariably when young). Sometimes, they lacked the understanding of how to retain their integrity while performing in show business.

It is interesting to examine how Celia Cruz, for instance, operating within Latin dance music, achieved this. With the combination of her tight, low-cut dresses, high heels, heavy make-up and fashionable wigs, and her fast sinuous dancing in the style of African traditions, Celia unambiguously presented herself as a thoroughly sexual woman (and in private, a bawdy joker with the dirtiest cackle). As a black woman, she was additionally laden with the implications of sexual potency and availability. But her expression of her sexuality has always been, in retrospect, measured.

Right from the start, Celia presented herself as the sensual elder sister, sexy but unavailable. She tells how when she first began, she never stayed out late – she would sing her songs, do the show, and then get the bus home. When she auditioned in Havana in the 1930s for the all-male orchestra La Sonora Matancera, she took her cousin along as chaperone. When she got the job, her cousin went too – travelling with her for several years. She says this was essential if she wanted to remain respected and scandal-free. When she began a romance with the band's trumpeter, Pedro Knight, they kept it a secret until they married, when Pedro – one of Havana's most brilliant trumpeters – sacrificed his own career to be her permanent 'chaperone' and manager. He still fulfils these roles, fifty years later. So Celia was protected from any possible misinterpretation; her sexual potency was transformed by making it obvious she was unavailable.

By contrast, a Cuban woman who tragically failed to maintain her position in salsa was La Lupe (Lupe Yoli), a contemporary of Celia Cruz, with a similar family background in the slums of Havana. During the 1940s and 1950s, La Lupe was resident in a smokey, bohemian nightclub in downtown Havana, Club Red. At the same time, Celia Cruz sang at the fabulous, open-air cabaret-casino, La Tropicana. She had broken the colour bar, which was in operation there and in most of the clubs where American tourists flocked for the legendary night-life.

In contrast to Celia's sexy but safe elder sister image, La Lupe was a wild earth creature, a kind of Cuban Eartha Kitt. While she performed in sheath-skirts and long wild wigs similar to those of Celia Cruz, when La Lupe spun and gyrated around the stage, possessed, purring and shrieking, she really was abandoned, and, by implication, available. Even more crucially, her life offstage was as wildly undisciplined as her art, and she suffered for it. Revolutionary Cuba was no place for either woman. After she fled to New York around 1959, La Lupe was an instant hit in the crossover between black and Latin music. She was known as 'The Queen of Latin Soul', with several record hits, albeit briefly, in the American market. But rumours and scandals about her tempestuous love affairs with respected salsa musicians and band leaders affected her work prospects, and her wild life and publicly unstable relationships, then problems with drugs, housing and bringing up two children, all contributed to a tragic decline.

In later life, she became involved in the Cuban cult religion, *santeria*, and eventually Christianity, but she died in the early 1990s, neglected and isolated in a home in Brooklyn. Her life had a certain Monroesque quality, without anchoring relationships to underpin the release of her creative brilliance through the stage and recording studio.

On a typical salsa stage, anywhere in Latin America, lines of men in shiny suits and flamboyant shirts parody and exaggerate the postures of macho manhood. Women are conjured up through song lyrics as adoring or rejecting characters, and appear on record sleeves in bikinis and cutaway dresses, draped around the musicians' waists like limp accessories. However, there have always been a handful of female musicians. In 1930s Havana there was even a short-lived craze for all-women orchestras. It started with Ensueño, and was carried on by the Orquesta Anacaona: the creation of seven Castro sisters bored with the restrictions of the house arrest lifestyle imposed on upper-class girls at that time. Anacaona played live concerts in an open-air café in Havana, and their success lasted about twenty years – the band acting as a nursery for many musicians and singers, who went on to success in male orchestras. They never really achieved a status beyond that of unthreatening novelty, but their very existence was something of a symbol at the time.

A modern-day equivalent of Anacaona was the merengue band, Las Chicas del Can (The Party Girls), formed in the Dominican Republic by writer/composer, Wilfrido Vargas, to match his boys' group, Los Hijos del Rey (The Sons of the King). Las Chicas, with their lacy tops, ruffly micro-skirts, clinging jeans and stilettos, and big hairdos were adored but never taken seriously. They mimed at their gigs; musically limited and hip-swivelling Belle Stars. I once saw them reveal the enormity of their lack of talent at a Miami salsa carnival when the power generator suddenly stopped and their horns were heard to be silent. But when the band split from Vargas, the trumpeter/leader Maria Acosta, and singers Miriam Cruz and Eunice Betances, brought in (female) musicians and re-organized the group – a move which then earned them greater respect and hit records. The lack of sexual reserve, and the explicit nature of their live shows, continued to imitate the conventions of the all-male merengue reviews.

In the 1980s, women's position in salsa began to change; I witnessed a micro-phenomenon of classically trained non-Hispanic women standing in the back line horn sections. For instance, the Dominican-New York band La Gran Manzana (The Big Apple) – a classic showcase for the three male singers, all gyrating hips, suggestive comments, and flashing smiles out front – featured a typical back line of horn players, except for a very serious, absolutely precise, slight American women. With her music degree, faltering Spanish and an obvious passion for the music which kept her constantly in work, she was clearly loved and respected by those same men who treated other women with predictably macho-blokish comedy.

Perhaps the place where it would be expected that women had an easier time in salsa is post-revolutionary Cuba. But on a visit there in 1986, I was firmly told by my guide that there was no need for feminism in Cuba: inequality was 'solved' by the revolution. So there were no women's bands and I saw no female musicians, only singers, in any of the tourist cabarets or nightclubs, where many of the singers who had stayed with the Revolution still worked. The majority of the post-Castro generation had joined the protest movement known as *nova trova* (new songs). Their songs, invariably accompanied by acoustic guitars, were a kind of throwback to the folksy-political civil rights song tradition of the 1960s USA.

A Communist version of Orquesta Anacaona (which was born at the height of Cuba's most repressive regime) has never emerged. However, in Miami today, the band run by guitarist, singer and songwriter, Albita Rodriguez, comes closest to that definition – and, in the way of things Cuban, manages to do it *outside* of Communist Cuba, in the heart of America. Albita, the daughter of two respected pre-revolutionary singers, was a central character in the *nova trova* movement in Havana. During the 1980s, Albita had spent much of each year travelling in Latin America and Eastern Europe, and her dedication to the country seemed total, until her sudden defection with her whole band via Latin America, to Miami. The band, which, exceptionally for Cuba, features a female flautist, mixes classic salsa songs with those containing carefully veiled allegorical lyrics about freedom and rights. As these do not exactly point the finger at Cuba, Miami Cubans can translate them in their way, and Albita can hold her head up in the support of Cuban nationalism, albeit from afar: a very model of pragmatism.

No discussion about women in the Latin world of music would be complete without mention of the most famous Miami export, Gloria Estefan, the Madonna of Latin pop. Gloria's reputation steadily grew through the 1980s, and now she has become one of the world's best-known artists, outselling at times Madonna, Prince *and* Michael Jackson. Even in an age of pop video with electronic effects and manipulation of images that would have been inconceivable to the young Celia Cruz in the 1940s, there are similar patterns in the two women's approaches to their careers. Having started out as a singer on the strictly Cuban-Miami scene, Gloria burst across into the non-Latin world of MTV rock with a stack of million-selling songs. Then, her position assured as far as is possible in pop business, she returned to her roots in 1993 with a potentially risky project of all-salsa songs, *Mi Tierra*. The album took her straight to the top of the UK charts, at a time when Celia Cruz was becoming known in the non-Latin world through songs with David Byrne and her singing role in the movie *Mambo Kings Play Songs of Love*.

In 1984, when Gloria Estefan was already a star in Latin America, but only known in the UK for the Miami Sound Machine singles, *Conga* and *Doctor Beat*, she talked to me about her transformation from shy girl into self-determined strong woman: 'When I was a kid, my mother used to push me to stand up at family gatherings. "Sing for us, Gloria", they'd all say. I used to sit there hunched over my guitar and sing, and never raise my head. I loved singing, but it was a hobby really, until I met Emilio.'[1]

She met Emilio Estefan, now her husband/manager, on the same family party circuit where she sang. He tried to persuade her to join his band, the Miami Latin Boys, and she eventually, reluctantly, went for an audition. Forty years after Celia Cruz had taken her cousin to an audition in Havana, here was this American citizen going along with her mother *and* grandmother as chaperones. They agreed to let her sing at weekends, while she studied for a psychology degree in the week. She recalls: 'When I first started with Emilio's band, I used to stand with my back against the wall, shaking a pair of maracas, and when it came to my turn to sing, I'd walk forward to the microphone, sing my song, and then get back to the wall as soon as possible! I was that shy.'[2]

Watching Gloria perform these days – in stadiums all across the world, on videos and live television shows – it's hard to tally such shyness with the supremely confident, elfin figure dancing around the stage, shifting effortlessly from uptempo salsa-rock to cooled-down ballads. She is also one of the most articulate interviewees. Always ready with jokes, she possesses that same combination of familiarity and intimacy which has endeared Celia Cruz to so many millions of people. The similarities between the two as performers and in the way they present themselves is uncannily close: perhaps Gloria has intuitively absorbed the Celia Cruz approach to stage presentation, audience relations and interview technique. Gloria has cultivated that same safe sexual power: she wears the skintight dresses and cutaway jeans, she dances raunchy salsa with her band on stage, but it is always obviously a costume, an act, discarded at the edge of the stage, rather than the lifestyle implied by Madonna or La Lupe. Added to that, there is the presence of the solid, supportive, ever-present husband/manager figure behind her. Emilio, like Pedro Knight, gave up performing to launch Gloria Estefan's solo career.

The Miami Sound Machine's sixteen-month world tour in 1990 served as a transformation for Gloria Estefan, as Emilio stayed home in Miami to look after their son, Nayib, and their new baby. The isolation and the experience of such long periods away from home and family had a strengthening effect on her as well as unexpected side effects. She says, 'It lead to a lot of gossip', laughing about it in retrospect. 'The big rumour was divorce, but I just ignored it. The Latin community can't fathom a marriage where the woman goes out and works and the man is at home, so they conjure up images of divorce.'[3]

'Wild Women' like La Lupe exist in all styles of popular music, of course, but they are usually deemed too dangerous to tolerate after the first flush of teenage rebellion is rubbed away. Nowhere was this more blatant than with the company director, film director, record producer, record label director, and singer/songwriter – Madonna. After she published the photo-essay *Sex*, and appeared in the film *In Bed with Madonna*, talking openly about her sexuality, she felt she was 'being punished'.

As she told the *Face* editor, Sheryl Garratt, this was 'for being a single female, for having power and being rich and saying the things I say, being a sexual creature – actually, not being any different from anyone else, but just *talking* about it'.[4]

Uninhibited female sexuality must be undermined, ridiculed, and ultimately destroyed. This is the modern-day equivalent of witch-hunting, though on the face of it the rock world tolerates – even encourages – more extreme lifestyles and performance behaviour than any other genre. But, as with punk and more recently grunge, the ultimate aim of the industry is to turn these pouting rebelles into passive yet saleable young women, once they have been allowed their fifteen minutes of banshee expression.

Few women have survived the rock world with their sexual potency intact. Possibly only Chrissie Hynde has continued to fly the flag for leather-clad rock'n'roll – and Siouxsie, Queen of the Goths, who continues to spawn new generations of sexually precocious gothettes. The majority of female rock'n'rollers do not sustain beyond their first decade as anything more meaningful than a self-parody.

But elsewhere in the world, and in cultures that appear to many Western observers restrictive for women, youth is not the hollow prize it appears in rock. There is still status in longevity and wisdom, and a woman's sexual attraction does not stop overnight at the turn of the third decade. Women like Celia Cruz, who survive the initial, admittedly tough, selection process, and with astute business management, can run and run, their status undiminished and even enhanced. Pretenders to their thrones, though, have a long wait in the wings: there is only one crown.

NOTES

1. Conversations with author between 1988 and 1993.
2. *Ibid.*
3. *Ibid.*
4. Madonna, interview in the *Face*, October 1994.

tell the truth

tell
the
truth

5 tell the truth

meeting margie hendrix

val wilmer

Taken for granted as the originators of most contemporary genres and styles, black entertainers have been a major part of the fabric of British music for over a century. More often than not, however, the social climate of the times meant that their offerings were tailored for whites; it was not until the 1960s that most British listeners were able to experience the authenticity of African-American vernacular performance. As an increasing variety of blues and gospel artists crossed the Atlantic in response to a growing demand for the Real Thing, the musical climate changed for ever.

A handful of blues instrumentalists and gospel singers had paved the way in the preceding decade, and as a teenage jazz fancier I rushed to hear them all. The only one I missed was guitarist Lonnie Johnson (he appeared at the Royal Festival Hall when I was only ten, although I did catch up with him subsequently). But by the turn of the decade I had seen and met some really legendary bluesmen. Big Bill Broonzy, Muddy Waters, Otis Spann, Josh White, Jimmie Rushing, Brownie McGhee and Sonny Terry – I still have the autographs and teenage snapshots to prove it. I'd also seen gospel artists Marie Knight and Brother John Sellers, the Eureka Jubilee and Clara Ward Singers, and been befriended by the guitar-playing creator of *Up Above My Head*, Sister Rosetta Tharpe. For me, as for many listeners of my generation, it was a musical education without equal and, as it later proved, an education in much more than the music.

Margie Hendrix, that was her name. Well it had been Majorie Hendricks on the early Ray Charles Atlantics, but that was how she was spelling it by the time we met. A while would pass before James Marshall Hendrix (no relation) emerged from his Seattle cocoon to straddle the world with his incandescent guitar and put that name on the map. Later still, Nona Hendryx of Labelle proclaimed her own version. But it was Margie, lead singer with Ray Charles's backing group the Raeletts, who broke the mould.

In Africa a child is named so that it may know its history. Disrespect for such naming traditions was a significant part of the process of enslavement that African peoples underwent in the New World. Just as family relationships were destroyed on the auction block, so rightful names would be snatched away and replaced by fanciful conceits such as Ptolemy, Dido or Cicero.

Not surprisingly, many African-Americans divested themselves of these as soon as they got the chance. They did not wait for the present-day Nation of Islam to advocate the wholesale replacement of slave-names by an 'X', they just grabbed a name from anywhere that had significance for them: a particular saviour, maybe – even a surname used on an adjacent plantation would do if conditions there were better than those they had experienced. The disruption of African family continuity has meant that names remain important in Afro-America; in a society that continues to call black people Aunt Mary and Uncle Sam, a name contains layers of meaning. Showbiz may have had a part to play in Margie's self-fashioned version but, like decades of Valaidas, Lavaidas, Lurleans and Lawandas, it gave her identity. Credibility, too.

But what did I know of such matters when our paths crossed on Ray Charles's first visit to England? It was May 1963, I was twenty-one and already a veteran of backstage encounters. Ray Charles, who was then creating something of a sensation in American jazz circles with his new 'gospelly' sound, had earned himself a reputation that positioned him well outside restrictive notions of 'pop'. Despite my awareness of this, I remained a jazz purist. For me, the members of his orchestra, most of whom were established instrumentalists, were the main attraction. I had met some of these men through photographing them on stage at the sound-check, and was not over-concerned, frankly, about getting to know the four women who provided the background for Ray's churchy vocals. As a 'serious' listener, I shared a view espoused on either side of the footlights – that the girls were just along for the glamour. Slap my wrists, but it's true.

Indeed, I doubt whether I would have met Margie and the other Raeletts if not for Michael Aldred, who had been at school with my brother. I ran across him backstage at what was then the Hammersmith Gaumont, a west London cinema, interviewing Jean King, the band's ballad singer. He wanted some photographs so I dragged myself away from the guys to oblige.

Jean took us to meet the Raeletts and 'motherly' Gwen Berry invited us to stay. Gwen, light-skinned, petite and as round as her surname, was the only one who kept in touch later, with Christmas cards. The other two, Darlene McRae and Pat Mosely, remain shadowy figures at the periphery of memory, demurely changing into diaphanous green affairs in the corner of a postage-stamp dressing-room.

Demure, Margie was not. Some backstage drama was in progress when she strode in, coat slung defiantly across her shoulders, and gave us a look that sent the temperature up by quite a few notches. As time went by I would discover that in most backstage scenarios there is one person who welcomes visitors, another who is excluding. Margie was one of the latter. She turned her back on us and 'talked black' to the others. It was really 'down' stuff, much of which we could only barely grasp the significance of back then. And yet, looking back on it now, the experience was in itself an education. To be treated as invisible and made to feel ignorant was preparation for understanding the situation of marginalized others. I have never forgotten that moment just as I have never forgotten Margie herself.

Her hairdo, as I can recall when I look at the photographs I took, was an outrageous creation of wigs and switches, piled high. As she sat at the mirror, combing some vicious sideburns into place, the air fairly crackled. Gwen, bless her, worked hard to get things back on an even keel until Margie calmed down. She could see that Michael and I were no trouble makers, for it was obvious that we had been accepted, and so, when I plucked up the courage to ask her to pose for a photo, she switched on a devastating smile.

When showtime came around, Gwen got us into the pit in front of the stage for the second house, and, with no one else between us and the footlights, we immediately felt part of the action. Encounters with music are quite different now, everything being so heavily amplified, but, back then, to experience the sheer physicality of a big band's instrumental attack was amazing. Brass and saxophones came together in fat, greasy riffs that built up tension across a funky beat; the sound hit our bodies and left us quite breathless. When the Raeletts appeared they acknowledged the applause, and then, to my great surprise, looked down and grinned at us where we sat.

It was then that the whole picture changed. Essential to Ray Charles's musical methodology was the African-rooted call-and-response pattern. Now, there was nothing special about this, the procedure is found in all forms of black music. But what Ray had achieved meant taking a walk on dangerous ground. The church was the place where moments of the greatest musical intensity occurred and, when Ray went there for his material as well as his inspiration, he broke some ancient taboos. He got flak from conservative blacks for translating the sacred into the secular, but he was the first to do so, predating Aretha Franklin and changing the face of popular music as a result. Back then, though, I had had little first-hand experience of black religious practice. A brief encounter with an American spiritual group called the Eureka Jubilee Singers had been followed by a jazz club appearance featuring the spectacular Clara Ward Singers. There had been concerts, too, by the solo performers Sister Rosetta Tharpe and Brother John Sellers. All were memorable but this was mere toe-in-the-water stuff. I was to find that I had a great deal to learn. And yet I knew what the Raeletts were doing. Taking their cue from Preacher Ray, they were doing what black women had done in the church from its earliest days. They were telling their story. They were testifying.

At the centre of these vocal exchanges, Margie shimmered. Her voice shook with vibrato just like one of the horns. She growled, deep in her throat, and contrived to convert the flimsiest chart material into something profound. All the passion she had displayed backstage came out in her music. She was scorching, searing, burning. And I was turned inside out and drained.

I could not keep my eyes off Margie; she was finding it hard to keep a straight face as well. That the Ray Charles organization brooked no insubordination from its musicians was well-known; fines for unpunctuality and infringement of dress codes were handed out with regularity. Whatever they might get up to away from the public eye, there were strict standards of on-stage behaviour, yet that didn't stop Margie from winking at us as we sat in the pit, even, at one point, bursting out laughing as we clapped on the offbeat. The fact of the matter was that all black musics thrive on response, and when performers are denied this essential element, they feel cheated. Communality, reassurance and affirmation are the staples, and the Raeletts had told us their first London audience had treated them coldly. I suppose they must have found some kind of humanity in our enthusiasm, something that had been missing at the earlier concert, but really we were just two kids, fans at their feet.

Of course I was in love. In love with music and with Margie herself. But for me she was about far more than her wonderful voice and her passionate interaction with Ray. Through her attitude alone and her obvious refusal to conform, she turned the table on every received notion of women's inferiority and black subservience that up until then had damaged my life. The lessons she taught have stayed with me always.

I never had a chance to interview Margie or to see her again. Really I knew very little about her other than what Ray Charles had to say in his no-punches-pulled autobiography *Brother Ray*. There he relates how he met the Raeletts, then known as The Cookies, at a Philadelphia concert in 1957. They were singing back-up for another great rhythm and blues singer, Chuck Willis, with one mike between them, and yet each part was audible, with no single voice drowning another. They were no strangers to the recording studios, having already made several singles, and Ray persuaded them to take part in his next Atlantic date – to leave Willis and join him and his band on the road.

A consummate musician who had carefully organized his bandsmen to give him the sound he wanted, he now did the same with the women's voices. He wrote parts for them, giving each a solo feature, and revelled in having their sound all around each day. 'I liked that male/female friction, and once I had it, I never let it go.' As for Margie, 'She sang even better than I had guessed. I tried her out on different things and she knocked me out. Had that growling, churchy feeling in her voice that I couldn't resist.'

Brother Ray is exceptional among musical autobiographies. The author recounts with some candour the 'droits de seigneur' he enjoyed with some of his singers, but he makes it clear that it was not only in terms of their musical rapport that his relationship with Margie was different. I was not surprised to read that in 1959 they had had a baby together. Recalling the electricity they generated on stage in their seamless exchanges, and listening to the records, I realize they had been 'doing it' on stage.

With the benefit of hindsight, it is easy to attribute too much significance to the particular moment. Autobiography is filled with such dishonesty. But I do know that I imbibed a lesson for the future at Margie's feet. Nor am I alone in this feeling. There is no coincidence in the fact that the music of New World Africans has been responsible for changing a great many lives, for its profound qualities and the message that it carries are linked directly with the life-force of its exponents. Poet Kate Rushin, herself African-American, went to the music when she wanted a suitable term for the female antecedents she credits with nurturing a nation. 'The Black Back-ups', she called them, simultaneously acknowledging generations of Margies, Fontellas and Dionnes, 'do-woppers' all, who had stood on the sidelines.

In writing about Margie, I have attempted a similar parallel. The music that nurtured me spiritually and fed me, was equally responsible for setting me on the road to wider understanding. I have always wanted to pay tribute to the first singer to set my soul on fire, and I have tried to trace the outcome of her story. Like too many musical tales, it is not positive. When she left Ray Charles's band in 1964, their relationship ended. He continued to support their son; but, musically, she drifted into obscurity. At some point in the following decade she died, mourned by her former lover but little heralded by the music community. In a 'starry-eyed' world she was 'only a back up singer', nothing more. But for those of us who have hung on her every musical nuance, who know what her voice was able to do, the story is different. Margie Hendrix, respect is due.

NOTES

Ray Charles's records are not always available, but a little detective work should locate two indispensable sessions. Both are 'live': the 1958 *Ray Charles at Newport* on which Margie makes memorable contributions to *The Right Time* and *Talking 'Bout You*; and the 1959 *Ray Charles in Person*, cut at an Atlanta concert, where her appearance on *Tell the Truth* (coming hard on the heels of Ray's own *tour de force*, *Drown in My Own Tears*) will ensure that your life will never be the same again.

Chapter Five first appeared in a slightly different forrn in *Second Shift*, to whom ackowledgement is due.

Trumpet section of "Ivy Benson All Girls Orchestra".
Left to right: Dorothy Burgess, Gracie Cole, Sylvia England.
The picture was taken during a summer season at Butlin's holiday camp in June 1949 and was later used as a publicity picture for the Besson New Creation Trumpet.

sisters of swing

sisters of swing

stardom, segregation and 1940s/50s pop

lucy o'brien

> **We were always a novelty. They made me leader. I was easy going but I didn't take any foolishness or give any. I demanded everyone be beautiful; fix yourself up, look nice, be glamorous and play. We were squares. We went to church on Sunday, we didn't smoke or drink. Other girl groups would ask us, what are you trying to prove? We weren't trying to prove anything other than we could play.**

Sarah McLawler, the female bandleader most famous for her late 1940s all-girl combo The Syn-coettes, plays regular nights at the Novotel in 1990s mid-town Manhattan. She has sparkling eyes, a wide knowing smile, a hat with ribbons, and a hand full of rings. Exuding the relaxation of an industry trouper, she scorns the 'tone-deaf jerks' in the latter-day US record business, the bland leading the bland on a pop scene where, to McLawler, everyone sounds alike and no one knows how to work. 'My throat was closed, my hands was swollen', she says, 'On the chitlin' circuit [tough clubs in the American South] I'd play matinees and evening till two every morning. If you wanna break a group, send 'em to Atlantic City. *That's* work.'

McLawler's smile covers a fierce attitude. As a black woman she worked doubly hard in the 1940s and 1950s to establish her own bands and a support network for female musicians. She emerged in the swing era, when women singers were considered Big Band trinkets and the only real musicians were male. This was despite the record of top instrumentalists such as 'Jazz Wonder Child' Lil Hardin Armstrong, wife of Louis, who was house pianist at Decca and leader of male and female bands from the early 1930s; or trumpet player Valaida Snow, pianist Hazel Scott, and Blanch Calloway who led her 'Joy Boys' to stardom, but was continually passed over by Irving Mills's influential booking organization.

All-women bands have a rich and varied history. From the turn of the century there were female vaudeville troupes, ladies' jazz bands and all-women dance orchestras. In 1927 for instance, trumpeter Leora Meoux Henderson led her female ensemble with the billing: 'The Twelve Vampires – Twelve Girls Who Can Play Real Dance Music'. 1935 saw members of black women's jazz bands go on to play with the renowned International Sweethearts Of Rhythm, who dominated the women's dance band scene through the 1930s and 1940s. Women's bands were often formed in response to the problem of getting access to the male jazz world – yet they were dismissed as gimmicks or novelty acts. Sometimes women caved in to the pressure, emphasizing physical allure over musicianship, as in one group who billed themselves 'The Band With A Bosom'. This tricky balance between stereotype and the business of playing instruments meant that many female musicians stayed away from all-women outfits as a professional tactic. Oft-compared to Artie Shaw, clarinettist Ann Dupont, for instance, led all-male groups from 1939, after announcing she was through with women's bands.

Taking a more positive view, McLawler says: 'I decided to help women all I could – whatever way I could help younger women, to inspire them.' A Kentucky-born child prodigy who began playing piano at six, later winning scholarships to Jordan Conservatory and Chicago's Fisk University, she began entertaining as a teenager in the early 1940s, travelling the South with her father's permission in Lucky Millinder's band. 'I was a skinny brat. Had me an organdy dress with yellow and a ribbon; a sweet little girl featured with the big old guys. They protected me, told me to eat my vitamins. In the 1940s then showbiz was very glamorous. All the clubs had chorus lines, dancers, comedians and complete productions.'

This experience proved very useful. On moving to Chicago to join her sister, she worked as a songwriter. McLawler would play at a cocktail lounge in State Street, doing 'double duty' because she was broke. 'I liked to play at night with the gamblers and big money people. I'd be riding the subway home at four in the morning with pockets full of money praying Please God, let me get home safely.' After some years as a 'single', McLawler decided to form an all-woman small combo. 'There were lots of girls in big bands like the Sweet Hearts Of Rhythm, but none out there expounding on their instruments like Dizzy or Miles in small groups. I heard about a new club opening uptown on the Southside, called Blue Heaven, and talked the manager into bringing in girl musicians to kick the place up.'

Leading some of the finest all-women combos of the day, McLawler drew talent from all-black bands such as the Darlings Of Rhythm and the Harlem Playgirls. Her famous Syn-coettes played as a top draw in Chicago and New York from 1948–53 before the momentum faltered when one of her best members, tenor saxophonist Lula Roberts, died of spiral meningitis, and McLawler found her hard to replace. Discouraged at the number of women who could not really play, McLawler worked as a single before teaming up with her husband, the violinist Richard Otto, until his death in 1979.

When I met her in 1994 at the Novotel in New York, McLawler was playing an array of jazz and popular standards and – true to her word about encouraging other women – she invited a young female horn player, Deborah Sandoval-Thurlow, to join her for a few numbers. Although McLawler and her 1940s combos were treated with respect by other musicians, she feels that they never got the critical recognition they deserved. 'It made no difference how good we were, we were always seen as a novelty. I've not been recognized for the work and the pioneering I've done.'

Despite a few individuals who managed to break through, the bands of the swing era were normally no-go for women. For many, their only route into the business was through all-female ensembles, particularly in Britain.

'I still can't believe she's not here. I haven't taken her number out of my phone book, I can't', drummer Chrissie Lee told me shortly after the death of her former boss and mentor Ivy Benson, the legendary female bandleader who died in May 1993 after a long, embattled career. Ivy's story is unique in British show business. Although there have always been women's bands, from the early 1940s the Ivy Benson Band was one of the major routes for women instrumentalists into jazz and studio work in Britain. While women in the States were making inroads into jazz and swing through such major figures as Holiday and Fitzgerald, and female bands like the International Sweethearts of Rhythm, their British sisters were some way behind.

Until the 1940s, the main roles for women in popular music were either cloying or comic. Music-hall star and Rochdale lass Gracie Fields set the tone for the 1930s with a humorous, slightly gawky image; while during the 1940s Blitz, the blonde bouffanted Vera Lynn was the reassuring gal next door who soothed with such songs as *White Cliffs of Dover* and *We'll Meet Again*. Through her lively request programme *Sincerely Yours*, a radio link between men serving overseas and anxious families at home, Lynn was dubbed 'The Forces' Sweetheart'.

In the same way that World War Two opened up job opportunities for women through munitions work, so it created a space for women in the music business. A charismatic, forceful figure, Ivy Benson took advantage of the vacuum created briefly during the war when many male musicians were conscripted, slotting her girls into the job as the BBC's resident dance band. She also went on extensive ENSA (Entertainments National Services Association) dates in Europe and the Middle East, earning the distinction of performing more concerts to troops overseas than any other artist.

A great enabler, Benson said proudly: 'I took a girl from a pie factory once, and made her a bass guitarist.' Born in Leeds, the daughter of 'Digger' Benson, a trombonist with the Leeds Symphony Orchestra, Ivy was playing piano in working men's clubs at the age of eight, and sax with the local British Legion band at fourteen. After stints with Edna Croudfoot's Rhythm Girls and Teddy Joyce's Girl Friends, Ivy decided to branch out on her own. Determined to make a mark in popular music, she spotted a gap in the market – women – and took it much further than novelty status, creating a big band that was on a par with major male bands of the day. Hers was the Ivy League, a kind of music school for girls in an era when the 'weaker' sex were not expected to play anything stronger than parlour violin.

'There were girls before, but it's to do with the impact one makes. Suddenly one will come out of the blue – Ivy was that one. People will always remember what Ivy stood for, and the fact that she blazed a trail for them all.' So says Gracie Cole, a quiet, taciturn woman and dedicated musician who played lead trumpet with Benson in the 1940s before going on to form her own All Girl Orchestra.

Gracie had previously played with the Gloria Gaye Band which she joined in 1943. 'The first thing Ivy did when I joined the band was take me to London to Boosey & Hawkes, the most famous music shop in the world, and buy me a trumpet', says Cole, who until then had been a star cornet player in Northern brass bands. 'I didn't join Ivy until 1945, but she'd had her eye on me all along. She first wrote asking me to join her in 1940 when I was still on cornet. She said if it's good enough for Louis – it's good enough for me!' Like a mother hen, Benson took full responsibility for her 'girls'. When playing to troops during the war, sometimes the band would socialize in the officers' club after a concert.

'Ivy would go on the piano, play for atmosphere and a few requests. Boys would dance with girls, but at a certain time she'd put her hat on and say, "OK girls, we're ready!" She'd stand there and have us filing past like a roll call. There was no question of hanky panky – she was very strict, especially with the girls under sixteen.' Part of this gentle yet firm surveillance was to protect her own interests: it was always a source of disappointment to Benson that she kept losing good female players to marriage and pregnancy.

Although she nurtured talent, she knew when she had to let it go gracefully. 'One of the first things to remember . . . is certain instruments consider themselves very hard to replace and one is tempted to do anything to keep them, even spend sleepless nights. Do not let it happen to you.' Benson wrote this to Cole, when in the 1950s the latter decided to form a women's band and nervously wrote to her former employer for the name of a good drummer. 'Remember the only important person in the outfit is yourself, and you pay the salaries, and you call the tune.'

As well as the name of a drummer, Pat Sheridan, who did go on to join her band, Cole was cheered to receive a letter full of advice: ' "Don't make the same mistakes I did, love." You could hear her Yorkshire accent!' But after some successful tours with her female outfit, Cole soon noticed the lack of support when she went back to playing in male bands. Her time as the only woman in the Squadronnaires was truncated because one trumpet player in particular, Ron Simmonds, found it hard to play with a woman on lead.

'He criticized my playing, would chat to others and ignore me, as if I didn't exist', Cole recalls. 'I had to really control myself and my playing because I knew he'd have a ball if I cracked a note. It got to the point where I gave up rather than play in those conditions. He said later he was envious because I was a famous player while he was up-and-coming at the time, and that made him mad. He was prejudiced, pure and simple.'

Benson was a useful conduit for women keen to be serious instrumentalists. Sheila Tracy, a trombonist with Benson from 1956–58 who went on to form brass girl duo The Tracy Sisters, remembers her period with the band as invaluable. 'Ivy was a good leader because she was strict', she recalls, 'I was put on lead trombone one night. It came to the last number at one in the morning, and she brought out an arrangement of *Rose Marie* – it had a top C in it and I cracked it. It was a bit of a solo, and I cracked it! She came down on me like a ton of bricks. Next morning I got up and said "I'm handing in my notice."'[1] Despite the confrontation, it gave Tracy the added incentive to put her duo on the road, the experience with Benson giving her the poise and musicianship needed to cope with a challenging variety circuit.

Benson recognized women's need to be not only 'as good as' men but exceptional. Tracy, for instance, never wanted to play the 'acceptable' instruments for women. 'I was sitting in the orchestra as a Royal Academy student in the late 1940s, fourth desk of the second fiddle, scraping away, surrounded by women. I looked up at the brass where there wasn't a woman in sight; all men were sitting up there. I thought it'd be rather nice to sit up there.'

Don Lusher, a trombone player with many of the big bands, including Ted Heath, admits it was difficult for women instrumentalists to get work. 'We had nothing against having girls in a band ... but you've got to remember it was a pretty high standard in those days. And maybe it wasn't as fashionable for girls then.' Tracy recalls that the amount of prejudice against women was stifling. 'Women were rubbished then', she says. ' "She looks pretty, but don't expect her to play the same way as a man" – that was the attitude. It's not true today because there are so many good girl musicians now in colleges. In my day jazz was absolutely taboo.'

Benson got her break during the War, but it was hard won. As Tracy notes, 'When the BBC made Ivy their resident house band, all hell broke loose, because it was the plum job in the country. The male bandleaders didn't want to know her, they loathed her guts. And the reviews for the first broadcast were vitriolic.' Adored by the troops and the general public, Benson became a British star, more popular even than Vera Lynn. Although she could have capitalized on her popularity with US troops by going to America after the war, she stayed in Britain to consolidate her position. 'Then every door slammed in her face, and with the band circuit booked up, there was nowhere to go. A committee of bandleaders was set up and they all closed ranks, saying, "We're not having Ivy Benson in." She said, "Don't you want me in? Forget it, I don't want to be in!" '

Benson survived by playing American bases and holiday camps before returning to the main circuit by the 1950s. Until recently, much of her achievement has been overlooked, but her 1960 drummer Chrissie Lee was keeping the spirit alive well into the 1990s with her own sixteen-piece big band. 'I formed it after seeing a TV documentary on Ivy in the late 1980s', she said. 'I thought, we can't let this go.'

The Big Band era spawned a number of vocalists who later became the female stars of the 1950s. With the proliferation of TV and a newly expanding pop industry, The Look became all important. Lita Roza, singing star and British postwar pin-up, recalls: 'In 1943 I saw a film called

Orchestra Wives. I wore my hair like one of the stars, Ann Rutherford, parted in the middle and cascading down. She won the good-looking trumpet player George Montgomery that was in the Glenn Miller Band. I put myself right into that picture. Everything happened to me just like that. I got into the best band in the country, married a good-looking trumpet player and that was that. Pity it didn't end happily.'

By allowing them to do men's jobs, the Second World War may have temporarily given women a sense of freedom, but once 'the boys' came back they were manoeuvred out of the labour force back into the home. Because so many women became housewives again with a sense of reluctance, a role of domesticated femininity had to be sugared and heavily sold, whether it was through Doris Day's wholesome peroxide image on screen or the glamour and glitz of the pop world. Not wanting to be cast as a 'peaches-and-cream' big band bauble when she was working with Gene Krupa, singer Anita O'Day set a new trend for female singers on the road by wearing a shirt and big band jacket on stage instead of a gown. 'I want them to listen to me, not look at me, I want to be treated like another musician', she argued. Krupa allowed her to 'dress down' for concerts that were not in theatres or ballrooms, but for many years she was considered to be a 'mannish' lesbian, because she refused to be mere bandstand decoration.

The 'gown' question meant that women working in big bands were set apart from male musicians, inevitably breeding an atmosphere of suspicion. Although they had more work opportunities than women musicians, big band vocalists often felt they were there on male sufferance. It took guts to stay in a career that could be very isolating. Women had to work doubly hard to 'earn' their place. 'Musicians are strange' says Roza, 'they either like you or they don't. They've always considered female singers a boil on the face of God knows what, a necessary evil. I had a genuine rapport with them, probably because I wasn't a time waster – they know I was a professional, there to do a job. We got in and out. I never hung them up.'

Women in the music business have always had to be singular and self-aware to avoid stereotyping, but in the 1940s and 1950s, when roles were much more restricted, self-belief had to be even more unshakeable – a rare commodity. The first woman in the UK to get a chart Number One, with *How Much Is That Doggie In The Window*? in 1953 ('I sang that song once and I shall never sing it again; I was what you'd call "a sophisticated singer" '), Roza was cool and resourceful from the moment she walked unaccompanied into a pantomime audition in Liverpool at the age of eleven. It was her chutzpah that led her to the job as singer in the early 1950s for the top British big band, after she impressed the bandleader Ted Heath.

'I'd sent a demo to Ted and he invited me to audition one day when he was rehearsing his band at the London Palladium. After I sang he said, "How would you like to go on tonight?" I think he expected me to fall in a faint. I said, "I'd like it". I went home, got a cocktail dress and came back. I went on that night and according to all the trade papers, I stopped the show.' After leaving Ted Heath, Roza became a star in her own right, her smouldering half-Spanish eyes and robust yet silky vocals making her a favourite with pop audiences throughout the 1950s. Billed as 'The Girl with the Pin-Up Voice', Roza was voted by *Melody Maker* the Most Popular Girl Singer every year from 1951–56.

The image of flouncy gowns and glistening smiles belied a hardworking reality. Roza's experience of constant, exhausting touring was typical. In 1956 she ended up doing thirteen shows in one night, for instance, when performing for British troops stranded in Suez. 'I sang in garages, hotels, bars. I performed with my hair in pincurls. They didn't care as long as they were being entertained. It was a wonderful experience, but God was I drained – I was dead when I got back to Britain.'

Ivy Benson's band was a rare example of women musicians working in solidarity, but more often the experience was a lone female. Elaine Delmar, daughter of the famous black band leader Leslie 'Jiver' Hutchinson, recalled touring on the Northern club circuit at seventeen in the late 1950s, organizing her own itineraries. 'I'd do a gig and go home on the milk train. Sometimes I'd play two or three clubs a night. It makes today's audiences seem easy. I've had whole audiences crossing over the club to get their meat pies. There'd be lots of booze, lots of smoke and rowdiness – the chairman of the club would come on stage saying, "Come on, give a bit of support, give the poor cow a chance!" Dreadful.'

As economic restraints on touring big bands signalled the decline of the swing era, popular taste shifted to smaller 'combos' and individual artists, and there was greater pressure on women visibly to be stars. In the early pop industry, beauty was constructed in order to dazzle. 'In those days it was the sequined gowns with a very tight waist', recalls Delmar. 'I'd go to a dealer and buy them for £200, £300. They were made by a wonderful dressmaker. And these gowns were *built*. You had to have someone pull you into it. Beautiful workmanship. If you bought one it could last you ten years.' There was an element of bravado in how expensive a girl could get her dress, and the bigger the star the dearer the sequins. When British star

Alma Cogan first approached bandleader Ted Heath, his advice was: 'Remember two things. First, when you sing a song you must mean every word of it. Next, you must always dress beautifully.'

Cogan took this literally. Only in pop can a dress be such an Event. Cogan travelled in Rolls Royce cars that had to have space for her dresses. For an ATV *Sunday Night At The Palladium* appearance, she once wore a dress with 12,750 rhinestone and diamante beads embroidered into the bodice, and 250 yards of nylon tulle hemmed into the skirt. She also left the stage door one evening wearing a dress covered in green feathers, but by the time she had passed through 2,000 fans to get to the car, she did not have a feather left, having been plucked like a chicken. For the Royal Variety Performance in 1955, she was worried about upstaging the Queen with a vast mauve crinoline dress sporting 14,000 beads. Luckily Her Majesty congratulated her on the outfit.

In the USA, Peggy Lee was the bridge between the 'hip' era of white 1940s swing and its transmutation into 1950s pop, with her ice blonde hair, refreshing delivery and immortalization of sparse, seductive tension in the 1958 *Fever*. 'The 1950s were a big time for clothes', she once said with characteristic understatement. There is a picture on the bill poster for a New York Basin Street East engagement that illustrates this. The words 'Peggy's back' are set beside a dramatic shot of Lee turned away from the camera, with shining coiffured hair that reveals most of her bare back. With breathtaking directness it spells Glamour.

Peggy Lee may have epitomized the high glamour of the era, but she had access to the mainstream in a way that was denied a contemporary like Billie Holiday. Both began singing in the 1930s, but within two decades Lee had outstripped Holiday in terms of sales and public profile. The sequined girl star was very much a phenomenon of the white mainstream, with segregation of music marketing resulting in the relegation of black women to the 'race record' or R&B charts.

If an act was racially mixed, it was easier if the star was white. Marion Montgomery, for instance, was a Mississippi belle who worked the clubs of the American south, a white woman sometimes fronting an all-black band. 'It was the late 1950s, a black band, and I was very blonde at the time. It never occurred to me what a dichotomy this was – a blonde white girl singing with a very jet black band', she says. 'They were wonderful to me. I have to say I didn't actually *tour* with them. That would never do. I played with them in Atlanta, which has always been a very progressive city. Atlanta is one of the few cities that didn't have race riots when it was all happening.'

Billie Holiday, meanwhile, had a very different experience as a lone black woman singing for a white band when she joined Artie Shaw in 1938. While touring below the Mason-Dixie Line, Holiday would have to urinate in bushes while the white musicians could avail themselves of hotel restrooms. Audiences complained about a black singer with a white band, and ballroom managers would not allow Holiday to sit on stage between numbers. Shaw unhappily compromised by hiring a white singer, Helen Forrest, and keeping Holiday, but it was a financial strain. It is testimony to the musicians' high regard for Lady Day that they each contributed ten dollars a week towards her salary. Although Holiday's experience happened twenty years before Montgomery sang in Atlanta, the alienating, traumatic effect of segregation reverberated up to the 1960s civil rights movement and beyond.

It was when Holiday left Shaw's band in 1939 to open at the pioneering mixed-race club Café Society, that she first sang the Lewis Allen lynching poem *Strange Fruit*. Every time she sang it Holiday got an ecstatic reaction – but she remained bitter about the racism that isolated and demeaned her. In *New Orleans* for instance, her first Hollywood picture, she was reduced to playing the role of a maid caught redhanded by the angry mistress of the house singing at the piano. 'It was a real drag going to Hollywood and becoming a make-believe maid', she recalled in her autobiography *Lady Sings The Blues*. 'Maid was the pits.'

A long-term heroin addict, Holiday was regularly tailed by the narcotics police. A spell in Federal Reformatory through 1947 left her with a criminal record and a stigma that triggered a spiral of decline. Just before she died in 1959, she was actually arrested for possession and fingerprinted on her hospital bed. Many feel that Holiday would have been less badly treated had she been white. Jazz singer Annie Ross for instance, one of Holiday's friends who was with her to the end, told me that to know Holiday was 'frightening, emotional, wonderful, nerve-wracking. She was my idol and it was an honour to help her, look after her. She was a victim of the culture at the time. I'm sure there were many people in America then of a different class and colour able to take drugs and lead relatively normal lives – but her livelihood was taken away when they denied her a cabaret card.'

The segregation that dogged Holiday also had an impact on the early pop charts. 1950s rock'n'roll star Big Mama Thornton, for instance, had a Number One R&B hit in 1953 with *Hound Dog*, but her success was eclipsed three years later by Elvis Presley's version, which went into the Top Forty. Black female artists hardly skimmed these charts unless, like Lena Horne or Eartha Kitt, they were lighter-skinned. A big band singer and Hollywood star, Horne was the first black woman to fully 'cross over' into the international club cabaret scene. Vaudeville star Josephine Baker twenty years earlier had to go to Europe to succeed, while Horne, feted as the 'New Negro' of the Harlem Renaissance, was both street smart and a symbol of the rising black bourgeoisie. Her grandmother Cora Calhoun Horne was a militant suffragette and Urban League/NAACP (National Association for the Advancement of Coloured People) activist, who left a political legacy for the younger woman to emulate. Beginning her career as a singer/dancer at the Cotton Club in 1934, Horne toured with Noble Sissle and then recorded in small groups with leading swingers of the day like Teddy Wilson and Artie Shaw.

A complex heroine, she did not supply easy answers for either side of the racial divide. Her career suffered because she spoke out against prejudice, and married the white accompanist Lennie Hayton. During the 1960s, however, a more militant younger generation criticized the former wife of black boxer Joe Louis for selling out to the supper rooms. Horne's reply was to the point: 'I can't get up in a nightclub in a $1,000 dress and start singing *Let My People Go*.'

Eartha Kitt was an altogether racier proposition. Haunted by the memory of a cotton plantation owner who overshadowed her childhood with his grim catchphrase, 'Nigger's a fool, nigger's a fool' (a man who took on Brothers Grimm monster proportions in her rags-to-riches fairy tale), she was determined from an early age to reinvent herself as the epitome of class and cool. This became translated at the peak of her career as an insecure arrogance, but her antagonistic behaviour was the result of trying to control a world that, when she was a girl, so devastatingly controlled her.

When I interviewed her at New York's Carlisle Hotel in 1994, Kitt was slim, sixty-six years old, bright as a button and just as scary. Her ferocious cool arose from long negotiation with a show business in which a 'yella girl' never properly belonged. 'When my career took off in the 1950s it was difficult for women in general, but particularly brown-skinned women. The William Morris Agency said to me, "Yes, you're a beautiful, talented intelligent woman who's got everything going for you, but we didn't know what to do with you." '

Not white enough to be a mainstream commercial act, yet not black enough to slot into the emerging soul movement of the black community, Kitt fell between pedestals, fashioning a bizarre act that was half Cat-woman, half sultry striptease and with brilliantly humorous styling. Despite almost grudging agreement on the part of a series of major labels

(Capitol, MCA, RCA) to put out her material – 'record companies thought I was strange. They said my voice was too weird and nobody would accept it' – Kitt had huge hits with songs like *Uska Dara* (sung partly in Turkish), *C'est Si Bon*, *I Want To Be Evil* and *Santa Baby*.

Born Eartha Mae in 1928, a sharecropper's daughter in the backwoods of South Carolina, she was abandoned by her mother to an adoptive family who victimized her because of her light skin. Always the ugly 'yella girl', Kitt set out to prove herself attractive for the rest of her life. 'Yes, I was abused, used and accused, but you used it as manure to be constructive about yourself. I didn't fall by the wayside', she says. It was as if she turned early experiences of sexual abuse by her adoptive mother on to the world. Behind the feline sexuality of the Catwoman pose that made her famous lay an element of hostility and aggression – a camp, 'vamp' image that crackled against the conservatism of 1950s pop culture, and led Orson Welles to call her 'the most exciting woman in the world'.

Sent to live with an aunt in New York, the teenage Kitt left High School to become a seamstress in a Brooklyn factory. She inveigled her way into the Katherine Durham dance troupe, and ended up becoming a featured dancer, travelling through Europe and Mexico. Kitt was captivated by Europe's seeming cultural sophistication, far removed from the racist South where she had grown up. This manifested itself in the affectation of her voice, a haughty, playful purr that suited the exotica of her self-styled Eurasian temptress.

I Wanna Be Evil Kitt sang, and you believed it. Black girls could only be bad and make it sexy: Doris Day had to have a shadow, and Kitt was it – fulfilling the potent myth of black women as morally dubious and sexually adventurous. Her career in the States did not take off until her Broadway appearance in *New Faces* of 1952, in which she mixed sex with sharp humour. Her main means of promotion were through expensive night-clubs, movies, and TV talk shows. 'They called me the crème de la crème of café society – which meant that I was a rich man's entertainer.' Though her act was risqué, Kitt insisted that she never took her clothes off. 'Not for my job. I wore skimpy clothes as a dancer, and I'd strip off a gown to flex my muscles. I'd have a bikini brassière underneath to go into a dance number. I consider myself to be sensual rather than sexy. Sexy is something you act up. You wear décolleté dresses with bosoms hanging out, your belly button or derrière showing. That to me is not sexy, it's just vulgar.'

The 'Bad Girl' stance served her, while simultaneously limiting her. Although Kitt's celebrity status gave her access to philosophers and heads of state, from Albert Einstein to India's Prime Minister Nehru, when she denounced the Johnson administration's involvement in Vietnam, she was reputedly blacklisted by the FBI. Once her career peaked with the arrival of rock 'n' roll, she was pushed further into the cold in the 1960s when, like Lena Horne, she married a white man – businessman William McDonald. By the early 1990s Kitt was back in favour with the White House, using the opportunity of a gala dinner there to berate President Clinton about high taxation. Despite her dignified status though, she was never keen to be seen as an ambassador for the black community: 'I don't think in terms of black, white pink or green. Black people told me I was a yella girl and didn't belong to them, so I think in terms of American citizens in general.' Then, laughing uproariously, she adds, 'I'm not a groupie.'

By the end of the interview she had visibly softened. 'People call you tough when you're really just shy and timid', she says. 'You're afraid of being rejected. I can walk into a room and I'm so scared I give the impression of not enjoying it. After you get acquainted with a couple of people though, and they treat you all right, then it's fine.'

Kitt was probably the last star in the transition from the Big Band Era to modern pop. It was a crucial period for women in the way they fought issues of race and sex to establish a place for later female performers. Women instrumentalists laid the foundations – whether it was Sarah McLawler fighting novelty status with her Syn-coettes, or Ivy Benson battling with Big Band chauvinism, while the vocalists of the era, from Billie Holiday to Peggy Lee and Eartha Kitt, began to negotiate what it meant to be a modern female star. Long before the growth of a significant women's movement, they operated either in isolation or through ad hoc networks of female friendship and support. Their legacy has been a sense of strength, artistry and a gritty kind of grace. In the context of women's pop history, the Big Band girls should be accorded a special place.

NOTES

1. Conversation with author, New York, 1994.

All interviews for this chapter by the author in New York and London in 1993-94.

SELECTED BIBLIOGRAPHY

Sandra Caron, *Alma Cogan*: A *Memoir*, Bloomsbury, London, 1991.

Donald Clarke, *Wishing On The Moon* (*The Life and Times of Billie Holiday*), Penguin, London, 1994.

Linda Dahl, *Stormy Weather (The Music and Lives of a Century of Jazzwomen)*, Quartet, London, 1984.

James Haskins and Kathleen Benson, *Lena, A Biography of Lena Horne*, Scarborough House, USA, 1984 and 1991.

Billie Holiday, with William Duffy, *Lady Sings the Blues*, Doubleday, New York, 1956.

Peggy Lee, *Miss Peggy Lee*, Bloomsbury, London, 1990.

Gene Lees, *Singers and The Song*, OUP, New York, 1987.

where are the mothers in opera?

7 where are the mothers in opera?

jennifer barnes

Take a casual glance down the cast lists of many familiar operas and certain patterns begin to emerge. There will usually be a young, 'good' girl (generally a soprano), soon to be thrust into some appalling predicament. The male lead (variously a castrato, countertenor, tenor, or, occasionally, a baritone, depending on the century) will be in charge of rescuing her, but, paradoxically, is often instrumental in her downfall. In addition, there will be the scheming courtier or, conversely, the wise counsellor (baritone/bass), an older man with capacity for either cruelty or kindness. Their counterpart is either the young 'bad' woman or the harridan, allotted to the mezzo-soprano/alto. If the young opera heroine lives at home, there may also be a father. However, rather than protect his child, these men vacillate between extremes of tyranny and weakness, leaving little in between.[1]

Yet in opera after opera, there is one significant omission among the 'dramatis personae': most of the daughters in opera have no mother. Where is Dorabella and Fiordiligi's mother (*Così Fan Tutte*)? And Rosina in *Il Barbiere*? Amina (*La Sonnambula*), Rigoletto's Gilda, Mignon, Zerlina (*Fra Diavolo*), Charlotte (*Werther*), Senta (*Der Fliegender Holländer*), Elizabeth (*Tannhäuser*), Lulu?[2] None of these girls has any trace of a mother in her life. Why, while the aforementioned archetypes provide endless permutations to create story after story, does the mother so seldom exist? And, more worryingly, when a young mother and baby do appear in opera, why must they so frequently die?

I want to look here at the life (and sometimes death) of three young mothers. Each story is harrowing, perhaps all the more so because all three are based on historical facts or real events. One of the three girls begins the opera with a mother, but, before the end of Act I, she is summarily dismissed. The others have no mother at all.

Instead, these girls have a composer and a librettist, a sound parentage of sorts, and a duo who feel strongly about their parental rights. Frequently, writers and composers draw parallels between their work and giving birth. David Belasco, author of the play *Madame Butterfly*, when asked which of his works he loved the most replied:

> First born or latest, the fond father is, I suppose, most likely to designate as his favorite child the one which he has most recently held in his arms. So, at any rate, it is with me; my plays are the vagrant children of my love, the cherished darlings of my heart, and each one of them has been, in turn, my 'favorite' – while I have been laboring to bring it forth upon the stage.[3]

Richard Strauss similarly commented, 'To me, finished works are not dead, but living cares and joys, like children.'[4]

In co-opting the metaphor of childbirth, male authors see no discrepancy between the fervour of their feelings and their inability to actually bear children. On the contrary, childbirth and aspects of motherhood are coveted and, yes, romanticized by the male artist. However, there is a crucial difference between bearing children and creating works of art. The first involves total abnegation of oneself, the woman's body and mind asked to go beyond extremes to produce the child amid chaos and mess. While miraculously creative, the woman is not in control. Generating art, in contrast, demands reasoning, refining, reflection, and a host of other intellectual machinations absent during actual childbirth. The aim is to distil brilliance from chaos, and, while the author may feel that his work controls him, he will be judged on how well he controls his work. As Susan Gubar and Sandra Gilbert observe in *Madwoman in the Attic*, a study of nineteenth-century writers:

> For if the author/father is owner of his text and of his reader's attention, he is also owner/possessor of the subjects of his text, that is to say of those figures, scenes and events – those brain children – he has both incarnated in black and white and 'bound' in cloth or leather.[5]

In opera, when a mother and child relationship does exist, the mother rarely has that kind of 'authority'. In fact, when a mother and baby appear in an opera, almost without exception, one if not both of them will die. Each opera based on the Faust legend includes infanticide. Médée also kills her children. Mélisande dies soon after childbirth. Marie is murdered in *Wozzeck*, and the baby boy in Menotti's *The Consul* dies, rather incidentally, of cold and hunger, before his mother commits suicide. At this rate, it is no wonder there are so few mothers found in opera. What are opera composers and librettists trying to tell us?[6]

Janáček's *Jenůfa* is known as *Její Pastorkyňa* in Czech, which translates as *Her Stepdaughter*. Like so many opera heroines, Jenůfa's mother does not exist. Or maybe she did exist and subsequently died. No matter, she is not there. The libretto, rather unusually for an opera, comes from a play written by a woman, Gabriela Preissová.[7] The story takes place in a Moravian village at the turn of the century and makes depressing reading. However, its violence is genuine; the events are based on incidents Preissová read in the local newspaper.

Sixteen-year-old Jenůfa is loved by Laca but loves the fickle Števa, whose child she is carrying. Kostelnička, Jenůfa's stepmother, not realizing her stepdaughter is pregnant, forbids Jenůfa from marrying the drunken, immature Števa for a year. Jenůfa continues to scorn Laca. He slashes her face with a knife, hoping that if he destroys Števa's superficial feelings for Jenůfa, based on her rosy apple cheeks, she will come to care for him. Kostelnička hides Jenůfa in her home for five months, saying she has gone to Vienna. Eight days after the birth, Kostelnička, trying to resolve Jenůfa's future, drugs Jenůfa into a deep sleep. She summons Števa and quickly ascertains he will never marry Jenůfa as he was repulsed by her pregnancy and her ugly scar. He plans to marry the Mayor's daughter. Laca, still in love with Jenůfa, learns she has had a child by Števa. He is shaken. Kostelnička, believing that Laca will not marry Jenůfa encumbered with another man's child, tells him that the child has died. Caught in her own lie and while Jenůfa sleeps, she carries the child out of the house and drowns him by placing him under a hole in the ice. She tells Jenůfa, when she awakes, that she has been in a raging fever for two days, during which time the child has died. Jenůfa, incongruously, asks not a single question concerning her child's death. She then accepts a rather ill-timed marriage proposal from Laca. In the Third Act, just as the marriage of Laca and Jenůfa is to take place, the body of a frozen child is found in the stream. The villagers prepare to blame Jenůfa when Kostelnička suddenly confesses. Jenůfa, on realizing Kostelnička has murdered her child says only 'Oh, mother, under the ice?'[8] (Act III, scene 10), yet moments later has forgiven her.

Despite the previous events, the final scene of the opera unites Laca and Jenůfa, now overcome with the deepness of their new-found love. As The Earl of Harewood comments in *Kobbé's Opera Book*:

> She is grateful to him for his greatness of spirit, and readily forgives him for the injury he did her; love for her was at the back of it, just as love was the cause of her own sin. Laca begs to be allowed to remain at her side, and his reward is Jenůfa's great cry of exultation as she understands that their sufferings have brought them a greater love than she has ever known. This is not just a conventional happy ending. The music has a freshness of its own, and the quality of Laca's devotion is pointed up by situation and music alike.[9]

But we, the audience, have been left with a problem. For the ending to even approach a 'conventional happy ending', we would have to accept, without flinching, that the mutilation of Jenůfa's face and the murder of her child were both events from which Jenůfa could readily recover. Laca means to wound her. Her jagged scar will be a permanent reminder of his capacity for violence. Števa also literally disfigures Jenůfa, but her pregnancy, much as today, will become branded solely as Jenůfa's sin.

Furthermore, Jenůfa's capacity to forgive (an element invented by Preissová), following the revelation of her child's murder, must be questioned. Jenůfa has trusted Kostelnička as her mother, and, to Preissová's credit, her betrayal is subtly yet meticulously recorded in the libretto. Throughout the opera Jenůfa incessantly calls Kostelnička 'mamicko' (mother), even up to her shocked, 'O mother, under the ice . . . '. However, in her act of forgiveness she commands, 'Stand up, step-mother!', and the devastated Kostelnička acknowledges the biological distinction saying, 'You could not inherit my character or my blood.'[10]

Yet amid this wretched chaos, while her child remains unburied and Kostelnička is dragged away to the courts, Janáček writes ecstatic music of overwhelming beauty for Jenůfa and Laca, as they pledge their love to each other. The final scene is extraordinarily moving; but can Janáček's music sweep aside the preceding violence to resolve Jenůfa's pain?

Jenůfa, the character, had no mother, but the opera was composed by a father who had just lost his second child. When referring to *Jenůfa*, Janácek remembers the time of composition thus: 'I would tie up *Jenůfa* with the black ribbon of the long illness, pain and cries of my daughter Olga and my little boy Vladimir.'[11] (Vladimir had died of scarlet fever at the age of two). As Janáček composed *Jenůfa*, he was also confronting the painful progress of Olga's illness. He dedicated the opera to her and made no secret of the fact that he based the character of Jenůfa on Olga: 'The more sick Oluska became, the more obsessed she became with her father's new opera. And sensitive as he was, he put his pain over Oluska into his work, the suffering of his daughter into Jenůfa's suffering.'[12]

On 22 February 1903 she begged her father to play her the completed opera, as she knew she would not live to hear it in the theatre. Four days later she died. The opera's beatific resolution is Janáček's courageous farewell to Olga. Janáček altered the ending of Preissová's play, which emphasized Jenůfa's fear of the upcoming trial and the loss of her child.[13] Instead, the final scene begins calmly, with Jenůfa's voice rippling over the orchestra. And as Laca and Jenůfa discover hope in their future, the phrases, like waves gathering strength, grow longer and higher, each more powerful than the last, until Jenůfa is able to say to Laca, 'Oh, come! Oh, come! The love that I feel for you in my heart tells me that God at last has smiled on us!'(Act III, scene 12).[14] In that moment, Janáček found the strength, if not to save Olga, to obliterate Jenůfa's pain. While Olga would die, Jenůfa would survive, even triumph over her circumstances. In his radiant postlude, Janáček goes beyond resolution. His faith in Jenůfa's future does not restore his daughter Olga; but through Jenůfa, Olga is reborn.

In 1904, the same year *Jenůfa* was given its première in Brno, Puccini's new opera *Madame Butterfly* was met by its first night audience with contempt and derision. Indeed, the shouts and catcalls often overwhelmed both the singers and the orchestra.[15] Based on a play by David Belasco, in turn based on a true story as told to John Luther Long, *Madame Butterfly* nonetheless struck the audience as a ridiculous tale told in a lurid manner. In 1892 there was indeed a Chô-San living high on a hill overlooking the harbour, who had given birth to a child by her American 'husband' and was subsequently abandoned.[16] It is believed that the real Chô-San's father died, or more specifically committed *hara-kiri*, following the humiliating defeat of the Samurai warriors in the Satsuma Rebellion of 1877. His act of defiance effectively left his family destitute. The fate of the historical Chô-San, once the proud daughter of a wealthy family, is unknown. However, the basic facts of her sad life, constantly embellished, provided both artistic acclaim and financial rewards for the several authors who 'adopted' her.

In John Luther Long's short story *Madame Butterfly*, one of the first things that Pinkerton does is forbid his bride Butterfly from seeing her relatives. He announces, 'I shall have to serve in the capacity of ancestors . . . and the real ones will have to go – or rather not come.'[17] Historically, it was not unusual for a daughter to separate from her family at the time of her marriage, in order to join her husband's family. She would then be expected to transfer filial love and duty from her real mother to her mother-in-law. But Pinkerton simply casts her adrift, with no family and no replacements.

By the 1870s, whether male or female, Japanese of high birth were discouraged from marrying Westerners. The American Clara Whitney recalled in her diary the night a wealthy Japanese man, having married a Westerner against his family's wishes, arrived at her family home in great agitation. On learning of the marriage:

> His father was very angry and immediately disowned him and compelled him to drop the family name and become a heimin [commoner] . . . . How great will her [his wife's] disappointment be when she learns the truth. But I suppose if I, like her had had no wise mother, I might have been in the same 'fix'.[18]

Not only do the Japanese (like the Americans) take a fierce pride in the purity of their family line, but we can also see that the young girl Clara had a mother whose authority both dominated and protected her. Yet in the opera, Butterfly's mother is depicted as dependent, too weak to stop her daughter marrying a Westerner; indeed, she must feign obsequious pleasure in meeting Pinkerton at the wedding, knowing she has no power to alter Butterfly's future.

The real Chô-San, when she realized her husband would not return (he had ceased payments on their rented house), abruptly left town, taking her child with her. As her death would leave her son abandoned, was suicide even a possibility? She simply disappeared. A most unoperatic ending.

Puccini's Butterfly kills herself, not only because she suddenly realizes that Pinkerton has betrayed her love, but, more crucially, because she learns he means to take away her child. This fictional aspect markedly changes Butterfly's situation. Puccini, who is often lambasted as being sadistic towards his heroines, insists on suicide for dramatic purposes, yet, in doing so, restores Butterfly to her full stature as the daughter of a warrior. Far from any sense of bowing to tradition, Butterfly angrily embraces it with music marked 'allegro vivace'. Consider this from *The Book of the Samurai*: 'Hara-kiri was always much more than merely a punishment. In many cases it was used as a very effective protest, or a way of proving loyalty.'[19] Hence, the fictional Butterfly kills herself, finding the anger to obliterate acquiescence, to finish defiantly. The strident orchestral postlude following Butterfly's suicide culminates in a final chord of crashing dissonance. In that one chord, Puccini both underscores and undermines. Butterfly's ending is a musical rebellion, an ending which should not have happened.

Over a decade later, Puccini found the story on which to base the mystical, spiritual opera he had always hoped to write. Giovacchino Forzano provided him with the libretti for both *Gianni Schicchi* and *Suor Angelica*, which, together with *Il Tabarro*, make up *Il Trittico*. While *Gianni Schicchi* remains a perennial favourite, from the beginning, *Suor Angelica* has been hounded by charges of cloying sentimentality.

Suor Angelica begins seven years after the entry of a former princess (now Suor Angelica) into the closed order of a convent. The first half of the opera establishes the quiet, resigned minutiae that make up the day to day life of the nuns. Excitement spreads quickly, however, when a carriage emblazoned with a royal crest arrives at the convent gates. Suor Angelica becomes particularly agitated, and we learn that for the first time in seven years her family has come to visit. 'Family' is in the form of the autocratic and unrelenting Principessa, the sister of Angelica's mother. From her we learn that, upon Angelica's parents' death, she was made guardian. She has come to obtain Angelica's signature on some documents, and, during this extraordinary confrontation, we learn that Angelica has disgraced herself and her family by bearing an illegitimate son. We only know that the child was taken away after one kiss following his birth. Now her aunt requires her to sign over her share of property to her younger sister. Angelica pleads for news of her son, and when the Principessa remains silent, becomes frantic. Like Kostelnička, the Principessa abruptly tells Angelica that her son caught a fever and died, but unlike Jenůfa, we immediately see that Angelica will never recover. After signing the papers, it is only a matter of time before she turns to the herbs she has been tending in the convent garden and poisons herself. But the opera does not end there. As she pleads with the last of her strength, Puccini ends with a vision – the Madonna appears to Angelica, and gently guides a young child who takes careful steps towards his mother. Angelica dies as he reaches her.

Since its première, commentators have consistently found the opera lacking. *Kobbé* dismissed it succinctly with 'The opera has never been popular.'[20] Erik Smith, in his sleeve notes for the 1962 Decca recording tried rather desperately to defend the opera: 'Though perhaps the least effective of the operas [in *Il Trittico*] . . . it in no way deserves the downright scorn meted out to it by an earlier generation, nor yet the apologetic and somewhat patronizing attitude which it is customary to adopt towards it today.' *The New Grove History of Opera* observes, 'Her tragedy obtrudes with lacerating force, culminating, however, on an unconvincing note of redemption.'[21] While Angelica's suicide is artistically condoned, her redemption causes critical alarm. In its early production history it was fashionable to praise the music but scorn the story;[22] now critical opinion has reversed. Recently, Julian Budden questioned 'whether Puccini rose adequately to the challenge of the culminating miracle, which ideally calls for the kind of transfiguration that lay outside his range'.[23] However, while few want to commit themselves in print, for many the opera is unbearably moving, the story and music commiserating in absolute symmetry.

On completing the opera, Puccini took the score to the convent of Vicapelago near Lucca, where his sister was the Mother Superior. There, with some misgivings, especially concerning the suicide scene, he played through the entire opera, singing the various parts. He later recalled in a letter:

> It was not easy ... still with as much tact and skill as I could summon, I explained it all. I saw many eyes that looked at me through tears. And when I came to the aria 'Madonna, Madonna, salvami per amor di mio figlio' ('Madonna, save me, for the love of my son') all the little nuns cried, with voices full of pity but firm in their decision, 'Yes, yes, poor thing!'[24]

Having colluded in Madame Butterfly's violent death, Puccini seems determined to allow Angelica a peaceful resolution.

Suor Angelica is set towards the end of the sixteenth century, but, apart from a reference to the Principessa's coach, has very little which confines it to that period. Written in 1916, it could easily be staged in the present, or at any other moment in time where a mother is forced to separate from her child. Claire Clairmont, the discarded mistress of Lord Byron and mother of Allegra wrote in her journal in 1821:

> Towards Wednesday morning I had a most distressing dream – that I received a letter which said that Allegra was ill and not likely to live. The dreadful grief I felt made awakening appear to me the most delightful sensation of ease in the world. Just so, I think, must the weary soul feel when it finds itself in Paradise, released from the trembling anguish of the world.[25]

Lord Byron had gained custody of Allegra and forbade Claire access. He then put Allegra, aged four, into a convent. Just over a year after Clairmont's journal entry, Allegra died in the convent from an unspecified illness. Unlike Angelica, we know that Claire Clairmont did not commit suicide, but lived out her life as a governess to other people's children. Edward John Trelawny chastised her in her later years for having such excessively bitter feelings towards Lord Byron.

Suor Angelica's suicide does not allow time for rancour and resentment. Instead, knowing that her son is in heaven, she prepares ecstatically to join him saying 'I die for him, and in heaven shall see him again.' Jenůfa, grieving at the news of her baby's death, says, 'So my child died, now he's an angel in heaven.' Before her suicide, Butterfly tells her son, 'My son, sent down from heaven, from Paradise descended . . . ' These utterances could be seen as almost formulaic expressions of love, but Claire Clairmont's journal entry suggests something more profound. For each of them, their child is their one link with heaven. Long before her daughter's death, Clairmont wrote directly to Byron, pleading, 'My dear Friend, I conjure you, do not make the world dark to me, as if my Allegra were dead.'[26] The ferocity of her feelings would not be out of place in an opera. Or is it that *Suor Angelica* dares to directly confront the strength of a mother's love?

Viewed with detachment, or, more pointedly, incomprehension, *Suor Angelica* suffers from the vantage point of its critics. In an opera that replaces romantic love with mother love, *Suor Angelica* searches for empathy and finds embarrassment. Moreover, while in an age of cynicism it would be tempting to cite divine intervention as the source of the problem, miracles 'per se' have been tolerated: commentators accept Amahl's miraculous healing at the end of Menotti's *Amahl and the Night Visitors*, and succumb to Berlioz's redemption scene at the climax of *La Damnation de Faust*, yet *Suor Angelica* continues to bear the stigmata of emotional excess.

We live in a time when film and television actresses fear reaching thirty, and exploitation means being yet another anonymous victim in a violent film. Janáček and Puccini involve their heroines within themes of violence and death, but in doing so create extraordinary, central roles for them. While the subject matter of each story is devastating, and a depressing commentary on womens' lives, it is to opera's credit – an art form often labelled as arcane and remote – that it looks unflinchingly at the darker issues surrounding mothers and babies. While much of history tacitly ignores the plight of women, these three operas confront their subject with detailed vehemence.

In bringing the most creative aspects of themselves and putting them before the public, both composers knew all too well what putting their children 'at risk' meant. On the day that the Prague Opera returned Janáček's score of *Jenůfa* with a blunt rejection, 'He sat at the writing desk. He buried his head in his hand and began to cry terribly. . . . That time at home was just like the return from Oluska's funeral.'[27] The death of a child, the death of a score. The composer, somewhere between the gestation of an idea and the completion of a project, has left behind the tempestuous days of creativity and has become the fiercely protective parent. He too feels possessive by birthright. Has this then meant that there is little emotional incentive for the composer in placing a mother between himself and his 'child'? Subconsciously, he may feel there is no room for a fictional mother, taking up time, notes and text, her very presence potentially wresting from him affection and obligation.[28]

In opera, mothers of babies are either losing their child or losing their life. Perhaps not so incidentally, most of the children born to opera mothers are male,[29] yet when the curtain rises on so many other operas, it is the young women, still living at home, but without their mother, who generate the story. These girls may grow into motherhood, but in opera it would seem a dangerous occupation. Moreover, who will be their role models? Does Rosina wonder how her mother would speak to the scheming Dr Bartolo? Does Gilda muse as to how her mother came to love the hunchback Rigoletto? Without their antecedents these and other opera heroines are free and yet at the same time lost – the world stretches out to meet them, and as they are pushed forward we say, 'Go forth, but I'm afraid there is no map.' And so they are left to wonder, in between arias, confrontations, crises, and resolutions, 'What was she like?'

Explaining the name 'Butterfly', the infatuated Pinkerton says to Butterfly, 'See, I have caught you . . . I hold you as you flutter. You're mine.' So too does the opera composer, without hesitation, love the child he has captured/created. But as any mother can testify, the need to completely possess must be confronted with compromise. She must watch the child, once a part of her own body, gradually mature and leave her. In contrast, the motherless opera heroine fulfills the needs of her spiritual father – she must rely forever entirely on him, and she will never grow up.

NOTES

1. For example, Ginevra's father in Handel's *Ariodante* and Lucia's father in Donizetti's *Lucia di Lammermoor* exemplify the cruel autocrat, while the fathers of both Cenerentola (*La Cenerentola*) or Sophie (*Der Rosenkavalier*) are simply ciphers.
2. I am referring to the heroines still young enough to be living amongst families or guardians. In addition to those named, a preliminary list would include: Angelina (*Cenerentola*), the title role in *Cendrillon*, Joan of Arc in both Rossini's *Giovanna D'Arco* and Tchaikovsky's *Maid of Orleans*, Anna (*La Dame Blanche*), Valentine (*Les Huguenots*), Marie (*La Fille du Régiment*, mother reappears), The

Goose (*Königskinder*), Antonia (*Les Contes d'Hoffmann*), the title roles in *La Wally* and *Iris*, Sophie (*Der Rosenkavalier*), Lisa (*Pique Dame*), the title role in *Iolantha*, and Tiny (*Paul Bunyan*).

3. David Belasco, *Six Plays*, Little, Brown and Company, Boston, 1928, p. 5.
4. *The Correspondence between Richard Strauss and Hugo von Hofmannstahl*, trans. H. Hammelmann and E. Osers, William Collins, London, 1961, p. 351.
5. Sandra M. Gilbert and Susan Gubar, *Madwoman in the Attic*, Yale University Press, New Haven and London, 1979, p. 7.
6. Opera mothers with children, rather than babies, show a different aspect of motherhood. The following children are put in emotional or physical danger because of their mothers: Pamina (*Die Zauberflöte*), Alceste's children, Norma's sons, Imogene's son (*Il Pirata*), Little Franz (*Intermezzo*), Hermione (*Die Ägyptische Helena*), Gennaro (*Lucretia Borgia*), Hänsel and Gretel, Louise (*Louise*), and Monica (*The Medium*). In contrast, Birtwistle's *Yan Tan Tethera* (1984) gives a uniquely intimate and positive portrayal of a mother in opera. Hannah gives birth in a matter-of-fact way to twin boys on stage and subsequently adopts two abandoned boys. However, in his earlier opera, a 'Dramatic Pastoral', *Down by the Greenwood Side* (1971), the character of Mrs Green relives the moment she stabbed her newborn twins. In the same way that Puccini reworks similar plots, Birtwistle's view of mothers and children evolves. Whereas Puccini changes the violence of Butterfly's suicide to redemption and reunion in *Suor Angelica* (albeit within the confines of death), in *Yan Tan Tethera* Birtwistle replaces the eerie, murdering Mrs Green with the nurturing Hannah.
7. In choosing Gabriela Preissová's play, *Její Pastorkyňa*, Janácek worked directly with the play's text, thus writing the first Czech prose opera (as opposed to verse). While he deleted dialogue and added folk songs, he schematically altered very little. The opera is still known as *Její Pastorkyna* in Czech, reflecting the structure of Preissová's play, which places Kostelnicka at the centre of the drama. However, the composer's influence is reflected in the fact that the opera became known in other countries by the name of the character that most inspired Janáček.
8. *Janáček: Jenůfa/Katya Kabanova, Opera Guide* 33, ed. Nicholas John, John Calder, London, 1985, p. 75.
9. The Earl of Harewood (ed.), *The Definitive Kobbé's Opera Book*, G.P. Putnam, New York, 1987, p. 1265.
10. *Opera Guide* 33, p. 76.
11. Bohumír Štědroň, *Leoš Janáček: Letters and Reminscences*, trans. Geraldine Thomsen, Artia, Prague, 1955, p. 98.

12. John Tyrrell, *Janáček's Opera, A Documentary Account*, Faber & Faber, London, 1992, p. 44.
13. Karel Brusak, 'Drama into a Libretto', in *Opera Guide* 33, p. 20.
14. *Opera Guide* 33, p. 77.
15. Mosco Carner, *Puccini: A Critical Biography*, 2nd edn., Duckworth, London, p. 139.
16. Arthur Groos, 'Madame Butterfly: the Story', *Cambridge Opera Journal*, vol. 3, no. 2, July, 1991, pp. 125–28.
17. John Luther Long, 'Madame Butterfly', in Nicholas John (ed.), *Puccini: Madame Butterfly, Opera Guide* 26, John Calder, London, 1984, p. 26.
18. M. William Steel and Tamiko Ichimata (eds.), *Clara's Diary: An American Girl in Meiji Japan*, Kodansah International, Tokyo, 1979, p. 207.
19. Stephen Turnbull, *The Book of the Samurai, the Warrior Class of Japan*, Arms and Armour, London, 1982, p. 33.
20. *Kobbé*, p. 972.
21. Julian Budden and John C G Waterhouse, 'Puccini and the period 1890–1910', in Stanley Sadie (ed.), *History of Opera: The New Grove Handbooks in Music*, Macmillan, London, 1989, p. 271.
22. For its British première, performed at the Royal Opera House, Covent Garden in 1920, the *Musical Times* recorded: 'The music is very fine, convincing in its atmosphere, and intensely dramatic at the proper time. But in England, at least, the convent is not well understood, and the listener is inclined to say 'Why?' to the whole business.' *Musical Times*, vol. 61, no. 930, 1920, p. 547.
23. Julian Budden, 'Suor Angelica', in Stanley Sadie (ed.), *The New Grove Dictionary of Opera*, Macmillan, London, 1992, vol. 4, pp. 601–3.
24. Guiseppe Adami, (ed.), *Letters of Puccini*, George G Harrap, London, 1931, p. 214.
25. Iris Origio, *A Measure of Love*, Jonathan Cape, London, 1957, p. 65.
26. Ibid., p. 68.
27. Tyrrell, *Janáček's Operas*, p. 50.
28. As yet, we do not have enough regularly performed operas by women composers either to justify removing the masculine pronoun or assess whether the mother would appear more frequently or develop any more significance. However, if we had an opera history generally dominated by women, in which the stories were repeatedly about the travails of young men, living at home, but invariably without any father or male role model, I trust it would come to the attention of musical, literary or historical scholars.
29. Mélisande's daughter, whose birth coincides with her mother's death, is a provocative and disturbing exception. It is as if Mélisande, who came from nowhere, and bears a child seemingly without the interference of either Golaud or Pelléas, has simply reproduced herself, to begin again the cycle of mystery.

full of eastern promise

full of eastern promise

women in south asian music

sairah awan

'You do not notice absence until it affects you.'[1] Sociologist Tessa Perkin's words rang clear as a bell when I began the relentless research for this chapter. Trying to find relevant and up-to-date material on South Asian women in Britain generally, let alone those involved in the music industry, was like trying to find a lost contact lens.

This chapter attempts to guide the reader into Asian culture from a woman's perspective, and to understand and demonstrate the conflicts between family, career and culture, which many Asian women go through in Britain. As an Asian woman, I hope this study will alleviate some of the misconceptions around Asian culture, and provide a better understanding of a group of women who are all too often represented as the passive victims of patriarchal oppression. This piece is also a celebration of Asian women's achievements and their contributions to the music business, but I cannot claim to give a complete and in-depth account, only to indicate an area which has been overlooked. I hope this will stimulate further research.

> Conjure up a picture of an Asian woman: what comes in your mind's eye? Have the words 'passive', 'submissive', been part of your portrayal? Have you imagined a woman beaten down and subjugated by the arranged marriage system – a woman ruled by wishes of her family – a woman not able to assert her own ambitions and desires – let alone fight against degradation and repression? If so this portrayal is a figment of your imagining. Racist imaginings which have taken strands from oppressive Hindu practices, imperialist ventures, capitalist projections and welded these into an inhumane whole which shackles us down.[2]

I am constantly told that I don't look, behave or dress like an Asian woman. This has more to do with my not conforming to the western stereotype quoted above than any rebellion against my racial, cultural and religious identity – an identity of which I am very proud. Becoming a music journalist was not something my parents had in mind for me (they had great hopes of me becoming a brain surgeon!). Initially, they were not ecstatic about my chosen career, especially with the lack of financial security for freelancers, my long and unsociable working hours, and concerns about my safety with the constant travelling to gigs and interviews. Nevertheless, they and the rest of my family support me 100 per cent, and have even mentioned (albeit very discreetly for fear of their daughter having a big head) being proud of me.

In fact it was some other members of the Pakistani community who turned up their noses. One girl in her mid twenties remarked, when she learned that I had got a job as an editorial assistant on a black music magazine, 'I thought you said you were going to get a "proper" job in journalism!' Music journalism was seen as inferior. The late nights coming back from gigs, interviews with musicians, and hardly ever being at home with my family had eventually, without my realizing it, marred my *izzat* (honour). I was seen as a deviant in my local community and a 'bad Muslim girl' who ideally should have pursued a career in medicine, law or business.

Marium, of Gangsta Bitchz – a collective of hip-hop and R&B DJs and promoters formed in October 1993 – comes from a family where the importance of education was particularly stressed. 'My mother is not the sort of person that wanted me to do law or business. [She] is very religious but has always said Islam is an open-minded religion.' Marium added, laughing, 'But I'm not sure if DJing comes within that! Although my mother is sick and tired of what I do, it's because of the travelling. Also because she knows that I get stressed out, because I'm always having arguments with people: trying to get money, props, and most importantly to get some appreciation, and so I've had a lot of fall-outs with promoters. I also got a bit of stick from Asian people for calling myself a "Bitch", but it's all part of the hip-hop scene.'

Radical Sister, a bhangra DJ and vocalist with the Derby-based band KKKings, also faced some parental dissent. 'Mum went bonkers when she first found out about [my] DJing. It was like, "How could you? This is not what you're supposed to do." And she chased me round the house with a rolling pin. I said, "I'm going to do it anyway, this is the 1990s." Then she saw me DJing at a gig and said, "Oh, is that all you do? That's all right then." Now she even calls me Radical!'

Sudha is a Manchester-based percussionist who has appeared on MTV. She has toured with Mercury Award-winning M People, and with K-Klass, Carleen Anderson, Corduroy and Kylie Minogue. She recalled: 'My grandmother came over from India and heard me practising some rhythms and said to my mum, "I'll leave her some money, get her a drum kit". I was only twelve. My mum was concerned about all the Asian aspect of things because she was a single parent. She sat down and said, "Convince me you're doing it for the right reasons . . . So long as I know exactly what time you're playing and what time you finish, I'll pick you up and drop you." I thought this was great', she laughed, 'cause I got a drum kit.'

Asian women are seen as symbols of their culture, at the core of family pride, which they have to uphold at all times by retaining modesty, self-respect and, most importantly, *never* bringing shame to the family. In Britain, *izzat* can still be as strong two or three generations on. With the music industry enveloped in notoriety and often associated with sex, drugs, and rock and roll, a woman's *izzat* is definitely at risk.

One way of maintaining women's honour is through *purdah*, a Persian word meaning curtain. Its aim is to preserve the woman's *izzat* and retain modesty and self-respect (*sharm*), both by concealing parts of the body through a dress code, and by physically separating men and women. Women in many Islamic countries wear some kind of veil. The extent to which they do this varies from country to country; in Saudi Arabia, for example, women are covered from head to foot in public. There the enforcement of this veiling system has been exploited and imposed by men as a cultural, rather than religious, phenomenon, so controlling women's sexual freedom and rights. The degree of *purdah* not only varies from country to country but even from one city to another, though *izzat* and *sharm* have to be maintained incessantly.

But it cannot be assumed that the veiling system is always a sign of oppression to all women, and it should not be cast as another social evil by the western world. In Britain, the *purdah* system still has a great influence, but the veil is now often worn through choice, commonly in the form of a headscarf. For these women, this symbolizes their devotion to Islam, and their defiance to a society which they see as antagonistic to the very essence of their religious identity.

In popular culture, men have been invited to look at Asian women. They have represented an image of the exotic through the achromatic practices of the *Kama Sutra*. The music industry thrives on such sexual imagery, and the title of this piece, *Full of Eastern Promise*, is an ironic play on this, evoking this eroticization of Asian women, but also reflecting their relatively untouched potential in the context of Britain's music industry.

Sheila Chandra appeared in the early 1980s, with her rock band Monsoon; accompanied by a marketing strategy which explicitly portrayed her as The Exotic Woman of the East.

Men are not immune from being portrayed in a sexualized way, but for women this may be the only way they are viewed. Sonya Aurora Madan from Echobelly makes this contrast: 'Men can get away with ugliness, or what would be considered to be ogre-like in women because looks aren't on the list of what's important in being a male.'[3]

Marium has challenged expectations. 'Initially we felt that [sexual imagery] was needed but now, no way! I dress down if anything. This genre of music expresses two types of dress styles, from the scantily clad woman to the very masculine look: chunky trainers, hoodies, baggy jeans where the crutch is almost by your knees, and big waistcoats.'

Contrary to popular belief, there are Muslim and Asian women who feel comfortable with their sexuality, but feel that expressing it in the explicit ways demanded by the Western music scene would go against everything they have been taught – and indeed value – about *izzat* and *sharm*.

It is difficult enough for any women to enter the music industry, and the experiences of those who do tends to reflect broader society's tendency to push women towards particular roles. They are often to be found in press and publicity, but few women work in management, or in technical areas like studio engineering and record production. If they are performers, they are usually vocalists rather than musicians.

However, there are women – and Asian women – pushing at these boundaries. Emteaz Hussain, a twenty-five-year-old dub poet from Sheffield, worked and toured with Benjamin Zephaniah last year. 'There don't seem to be that many Asian women', she said, 'and that's not because they aren't musical. The music industry does not accommodate our needs and culture, and their wide and diverse talents and contributions just don't get the recognition or support. But it's only a matter of time for breakthrough, as there is a lot of talent out there.'

Thirty-one-year-old DJ Ritu, who has been around the music scene for nearly ten years, has an impressive CV. A&R director of OutCaste Music and resident DJ at the Wag nightclub, London, she was the first Asian DJ on Kiss FM. As well as regular guest DJ slots at a number of major London clubs, she has appeared across the country and overseas – Toronto, Amsterdam, Vienna, Berlin, Tokyo – playing an array of house, garage, soul, swing, ragga, African, Arabic, Latin and Asian.

'I started in radio in 1986 and then worked my way through the lesbian/gay scene, and have now got involved on the Asian scene, but would like to go more mainstream', explained Ritu. 'When I first got involved in music, my family thought that it was another eccentricity of mine, but gave me a lot of support; and working on the BBC 3 County Radio [the first women-run station which had a two-week pilot licence] gave me more status. I'm going to continue DJ'ing in the clubs but . . . I'd like to move on to production and remix work. Hopefully I'll play a strong role in OutCaste Music. The music industry is still very male, you just have to prove yourself that much more. I have to be better to make a mark [but] I feel the time is right for Asian women to come through.'

Bushra Ahmed is an entrepreneur. A woman of the 1990s, her business skills as partner of Manchester-based Joe Bloggs have led her into artist management. Her act, twenty-four-year-old vocalist Sabina, presents Star TV, the biggest TV network in SE Asia, watched by over 2.5 billion viewers and owned by Rupert Murdoch. As well as touring through Europe and the Far East, Sabina has worked with Phil Chill, Mark Rutherford and Sugar Jay of Bassomatic on 'Fascinating Rhythm', and with Edwin Starr. She has her own show on Sunset Radio and has appeared on BPM, The Word and The Beat.

'Sabina made a tape which I heard and thought it was fantastic!' enthused Bushra. 'At that time I didn't have a clue about music but I decided that I wanted to be her manager. That's when I realized it's quite a serious role. Sabina didn't have the right image then and really didn't look the part, so it was a massive process to make her fit the bill, and I began moulding her. She couldn't survive in this shark-infested world where there's always someone ripping you off.'

The experiences of Asian women have often been examined through a Eurocentric feminist model, which ignores or is unable to take on the diversity of cultures in the sub continent. There is no homogenous Asian identity, and this can be seen in the way in which Asian women from different cultural and religious backgrounds have entered the music business. So far most of these have been Indian or Sikh. Muslim girls are least likely to be attracted to this field both for cultural and personal reasons.

As Marium said, 'I don't know that many Muslim sisters involved in music, but that may be because of the stereotypical attitudes that a Muslim woman has to act in this way or that way.' A woman's role as a wife has always been very important to Muslim families. But things are changing (and not just for Muslim women) as increasing numbers of Asian women enter higher education and go on to have professional careers in areas such as the arts and music.

> Careers are very important to Indian people which is good for women because things can be very equal in that way, but they have no appreciation of the arts. I think it's the same in any country where there's no social security ... To be an artist means you will have aesthetic value, but you won't have any monetary gain so you won't be on the same level as a doctor or a lawyer. Also Indian people came to England to find work.[4] [Sonya Aurora Maden]

Pinky (Parvinder Matharu), a mother of four, handles PR for Multimedia, who were signed by EMI Records in 1994, and she promotes up-and-coming Asian acts. In the past, Pinky has worked on Upna Beat, which originally started off as an Asian news and music publication covering issues often overlooked, such as the gay underground scene. She was also involved with Entasia, a promotion company renowned for hosting bhangra and DJ Awards. 'It was very hard being an Asian woman in the music industry', she said, 'and they were not sure how they would take to an Asian woman. But I feel I am one of the fortunate ones that has gained respect. I've worked hard and I'm proud of it. Although some Asian girls are suppressed by their parents, a lot more will eventually go into the music business. Kids are becoming more independent and parents are starting to come around. [But] it's all about contacts at the end of the day, which is sad, I know.'

> Of all the Black communities settled in Britain, it is the Asians who are viewed as the most Alien. The problems that Asians represent to the British way of life and culture, this threat to Britishness, is encapsulated in their difference, their unwillingness to adapt to change, their tendency to cling to their curries, their language, their way of dressing and above all their peculiar patterns of household organisations and gender relations.[5]

All races use their cultures and traditions to make sense of their lives. In their efforts to somehow fit into British society, blacks and Asians tend to do this more than their white peers. Their experiences of racism have confirmed to blacks and Asians that to be really English you should also be white. While black peoples' history has constantly been problematized and questioned, white identity has always been taken for granted as 'given'. Asian culture, whether expressed through music or identity, is far from accepted in western society, and Asians are still treated as inferior because of their social practices, 'weird' rituals and beliefs. Irish, Jews and Blacks have long suffered the brunt of racism in Britain, and it now appears to be the turn of Asian people, who, because of their stereotyped passive nature, are often seen as soft targets.

People of African and Caribbean origins can appear to be more integrated into British culture than Asians, because of apparent similarities in language and religious traditions. One of the ways in which Asians have assimilated into British society is by adopting black culture. Popular music has always been strongly influenced by black influences, and rap and dance is currently making big money within the industry. But Asian culture is relatively new in the West, and Asian melodies are distinctively different.

Bushra Ahmed, who manages Sabina, knows only too well that Asian identity could cost her artist her career. 'At the end of the day it's a job. Sabina loves what she does and she's not there to fly the flag for anybody although we would love to fly [it] for Asians. We'd want to throw it at them, but right now it could jeopardize everything. Apache Indian, Voodoo Queens, Echobelly and Kaliphz can't go around saying they're Asian. Those are the rules. If you don't follow them you might as well kiss it all goodbye.'

Nimisha is a twenty-year-old R&B vocalist who has performed at the ever popular, annual festival, the Streatham Common Mela, and at London clubs such as The Wag. She has worked with MC Raw, and recorded an album in 1995. Nimisha writes her own songs and dances with influences from Indian classical to ballet, to contemporary tap, to jazz.

'My parents have supported me 100 per cent', she said, 'I'm still very new to the music business, but have realized that it can be very vicious and you really have to look after yourself. At the beginning people looked at me and thought it was strange an Asian girl would want to sing soul music, but know I think they're getting used to seeing me perform. Within myself I'm an artist, not Asian, black, white or anything . . . I don't consciously compete with anyone but myself.'

However, Radical Sister feels very differently. 'The name KKKings is a swipe at the Ku Klux Klan and also to symbolize the 5 Ks of the Sikh religion (kara (comb), kunga (bangle), kesh (long hair), kachera (underpants) and kirpan (sword). The name was chosen quite seriously, basically to show where we're from and where we're going. It's a celebration of Asian culture, of being Asian in England.'

Where traditionally strong Asian images are not used, appearances can be very deceptive. Sudha found that many people did not think she was

Asian, 'Because of the way I look [short black hair and funky black-rimmed glasses], and the way I dress, I guess it takes away my Asianness and I get people asking me, "Are you French? Are you Spanish?" As if it's meant to be a compliment to be considered European rather than Asian!' Marium of Gangsta Bitchz believes, 'I don't look Asian, which helps because I'd get a lot of shit otherwise. I'm outspoken, and if people are ignorant I'll point it out.'

Some artists find that the stereotype of Asian women's passivity is used against them. Sudha again, 'The music industry stinks completely. I've been in it for a year and I think at the beginning of that year I was completely naive. I'd be like, "Don't worry about it, yes I'll have my money in a week's time ... Oh, a cheque is fine ... No, no, I won't need a contract." But now, I hardly ever do work for no money. I'm a lot more assertive. You know, things like having to phone up people and go, "Where's my money? When do you want me? How much are you paying me? Are you going to pay for a hired car? Have I got a hotel?" '

Some women have found themselves on the end of prejudice which can spill over into explicit racism. Manager Bushra Ahmed recalls, 'Something can't have been right. It's taken eight years to get Sabina off the ground. There's a lot of prejudice. Asian people should have a corner shop, Asian women should get married, and I was constantly told that an Asian artist wasn't right for their [record company's] image. There have been times where I have totally broken down. Sometimes we've both been depressed and have both cried. My parents thought I was being stupid and would say, "See I told you so", but that just put me on a mission to succeed – even if I spend the rest of my life trying. I won't stop until I succeed.'

Sudha recalls only one incident. 'This happened the second time I played with K-Klass in Liverpool. I was sitting down after having played, and a bouncer went up to the manager and said, "What's that Paki doing here?" '

Although Marium has not come across any direct racism, she does believe she has been on the end of it in more subtle forms. When she was promoting a night at a well-known nightclub, the management 'weren't keen and didn't want to take the "risk", although we had big names like Boogie Bunch and Rampage playing. To this day I will say that they were being racist.' However, she also feels, 'Being a female club promoter, you're not taken seriously, and a lot of guys are intimidated and don't like to see women in that position – that women can go and do exactly what they're doing.' But this is not always about racism. Marium continued, 'If anything, I think it's the Asian guys that have tried to be intimidating.

They've got a very strange attitude and can't seem to handle me. When I played at Limelight, an Asian DJ was determined to fuck it up and kept interrupting the set.'

Making a break in the music business is often all about knowing the right people, being in the right place at the right time, or just sheer luck. As outsiders, black and especially Asian musicians have had to demonstrate success in their local communities through pirate stations, using bootlegs (illegal sound recordings), before getting access to the mainstream. The music industry is driven by a fear of low profit margins, and is especially cautious when faced with what it sees to be untested and alien forms. As a result, traditional Asian music still remains predominately underground, sold exclusively in Asian shops. But bhangra, a more youth-orientated dance music, appears to be on the point of some sort of breakthrough to larger audiences, with opportunities for women singers such as Sangeeta and Vibha on Keda Records, and DJs like Radical Sister.

Bhangra is a folk music that fuses dance and song. It originates from the Punjab, a rich agricultural area, belonging to both India and Pakistan. The music is a powerful and vital symbol of community bonds and ties in the Punjab which have persisted in Britain. Bhangra is derived from *bhang*, an Urdu word for Indian hemp (cannabis), and expresses exactly what the celebrations achieved: a complete feeling of ecstasy from a successful harvest.

In the villages the only instrument used was the dhol: a large cylindrical drum, double-headed and usually made of wood played standing upright. It is the beat of this drum which gives bhangra its distinct style. The bhangra dance imitates the farmers' movements on the fields with emphasis on arms, shoulders and head, and the sweeping movements of the scythes, and it is the same style of dance that is still seen in clubs and functions today. When bhangra was introduced indoors, the dhol was replaced by the dholak – a smaller version of the dhol common to northern areas of India and Pakistan among performers such as the quwvali singers (singers of Muslim devotional music). It is also a domestic instrument played mainly by women, and it was on the dholak that they played songs to celebrate birth and wedding songs, which were passed down from the Mughal palaces.

After the war, when Britain recruited workers from its former colonies, a sigificant number were Sikhs. They brought with them bhangra, still in its raw and traditional form. They saw Britain as an alien and hostile country and they initially refrained from religious festivals, celebration of Vaisakhi[6] and birthdays, as it could draw attention and cause friction with their neighbours. But once these migrant workers were reunited with their families, the celebrations in Britain slowly began to emerge.

However, their children were attracted to other styles, especially reggae, soul and R&B, although this was to change. The vast majority of the first generation of British children born to Asian parents were caught between two cultures, and this caused much stress and anxiety. Many parents saw their children as rebellious, and accused them of throwing away their Asian identity and adopting a western one. The children felt their parents were old-fashioned and could not understand why they were so stuck in their ways.

By the 1980s, as American hip-hop began to influence the music scene, the youth started hiring small venues, such as back rooms of pubs and school halls, for parties. They were held in the day, as the young Asian girls would otherwise have been refused permission to go, to prevent their *izzat* from being harmed. Slowly bhangra began to trickle into these events, and the venues became more lavish as its popularity escalated. Eventually halls were hired, holding up to two thousand people, and the bhangra artists who originally performed at weddings and community events were now being hired at these clubs. Bhangra took over completely in the 1980s. However, the daytimes began to attract media attention as many students, especially girls, started missing school to attend.

DJ Ritu explains, 'It attracted a lot of media attention in 1986, with youths playing truant to attend these gigs. Daytimes were featured heavily in the tabloids and then dropped like a hot potato out of the blue. There was some trouble at one of the gigs, culminating in a fatal stabbing which temporarily halted the daytime bhangra scene. Parents didn't want their kids to go to these dos, and club promoters weren't keen to carry on.'

But in the 1990s we are witnessing a third generation of British Asians for whom many of the traditional cultural values have become diluted by a much more liberal stance. Daytimes have become less popular, being replaced by clubs and sell-out bhangra concerts. They still take place, but mainly in the North and Midlands, where Asian culture and traditions are stricter than in the south.

DJ Ritu described the London scene: 'Bombay Jungle at The Wag Club was put together by three different sound system promoters in September 1993. A weekly generous helping of bhangra and black music, catering for Asians that enjoy bhangra, and for those that don't, yet still want to be the majority rather than the minority race at a club night. Bombay Jungle is an exception, in that it's the first night for Asians run by Asians. Now bhangra is moving into other venues: the London Palais in Hammersmith, Kudos in Watford, but as yet these are still one-off events. Nevertheless the UK is *the* focal point for contemporary bhangra, which is now being shipped abroad – for the last four to five years, snowballing from country to country.'

The shared interest of young Asians in both black music and bhangra has been a significant factor in the music played at the daytimes in the 1980s and club nights in the 1990s. Both blacks and Asians are incorporating the two different cultures to their advantage, especially through fusions of music. The current generation of Asian youth have moulded bhangra into another variation. Its drumbeat has become the foundation of many tracks combining Asian melodies with almost every genre – folk, reggae, rap, hip-hop, and, more recently, jungle.

Many British Asian musicians have been influenced by bhangra as have non-Asian such as Loop Guru. Aki Nawaz (better known as Propa-Ghandi, former drummer of punk band The Cult) formed Fun-Da-Mental in 1991, recording for Nation Records, which he also runs. The band's melodic fusion of qavvali, bhangra, zikar and classical Indian music has blended sweetly with indie, hip-hop and radical political vocals, but they are perceived by some as overtly militant and offensive.

Chunni, lead vocalist of traditional bhangra band, Alaap, formed in the mid 1970s disagrees with such experimentation and does not class the music in the bhangra charts as proper bhangra. With the influence of reggae, ragga and hip-hop, 'it's becoming more of a black thing rather than an Asian thing', and he feels bhangra 'will totally lose its cultural values.'[7]

But Radical Sister disagrees, and feels that the music she plays with KKKings, 'a mixture of Hindi vocals, Punjabi and mellow chill out rap, is representative of the times we are living in, and that integrating all cultures is the way forward.' Traditional bhangra storytelling is quite light-hearted, romantic, but can also be quite sexist and patronizing to women. But KKKings, a band with women members, give bhangra lyrics a new slant, often dealing with more subversive issues, as in this song:

> Nau jawan [the new young man] came on a 747
> Cross seven seas to blighty heaven
> Killed some time in factory hell
> Saved his pennies for the wishing well
> Hah!! Look at him now off with the turban
> He wants to be suburban
> He's got to drink bourbon.[8]

The fast-changing nature of Asian music in Britain in all its forms from bhangra to rock is exciting. 'It's a clear-cut case of hybridity, borrowing from other cultures and not being rooted in one particular place', explained Ash Sharma, Lecturer at the University of East London. 'There have been quite a few changes in Asian culture in Britain, with the wearing of western clothes as compared to the first generation of women who will still wear salwar kameez or saris; the rising number of semi-arranged marriages, including partners of a different race, colour and creed; and career moves, and this has been reflected in music. . . . It's the Asianness of artists such as Sonya Aurora Madan from Echobelly and Voodoo Queens that makes them stand out, but their music culturally is very British.'

The Voodoo Queens' lyrics ooze revengeful passion and use a fusion of Hindi film music and indie rock in their track *Indian Filmstar*, while other songs make witty comments on handbags, and shopping. Sheila Chandra's 1994 album *Zen Kiss*, on Real World records, is a mixture of English melodies, crossed not just with Indian music, but with blues, gospel and techno, and is a perfect example of fusion or hybridity at its fullest.

There are many more Asian women involved in music than have been included here. But I felt that those I interviewed provided positive examples of success in their respective fields, as well as honesty about some of the difficulties.

Some artists refused to be included, which I found surprising. I cannot know whether Bushra Ahmed's blunt and honest comments on Asian women and identity crises in the music business are also representative of the feelings of those women who were reluctant to be included in a piece solely about Asian women (although they have appeared on numerous occasions in the mainstream popular music press).

The overall consensus of those I spoke to was that barriers still need to be broken down and more exposure granted to all things Asian. If Asian men are struggling in the music business, who is to say that Asian women will find it any easier? In recent years African-Caribbean style and fashion has been adopted by both whites and Asians, yet any widespread acceptance of Asian culture still seems a very long way off, and to some extent young Asians remain invisible in British society.

The music business has been guilty of tokenism in not treating Asian musicians' contributions as anything more than an occasional novelty; and of using tired old fantasies to exoticize Asian women artists. And while there is a widely held assumption that all Asians have one culture, religion and language, how can Asian people ever really be understood and taken seriously? It is hardly surprising that whenever an Asian artist uses some kind of musical influence from the Indian subcontinent, bhangra is usually the label applied, even though there are many kinds of Asian music. (It is true that I have concentrated on bhangra here, as it is currently the most influential Asian music for young people. But Hindi film music has also been significant, and an important factor in the development of Asian communities in Britain.)

Those women who have had achievements in the music business should be seen and respected as providing role models for the next generation of young British Asian women. Despite the many cultural, racial and sexual barriers, Asian women are emerging in all areas of the industry and, in Imteaz Hussain's words, 'Watch out, here we come!'

THANKS

Orson Nava. You're a star! Love the Artful Dodger.
Also thanks to Pete 'Mac Master' Chalk, Tas Awan, Marie Caliendo, Kam-Mee Li, Danny Broderick and, last but not least, my flatmate Gabby Zegge.

NOTES

1. Lecture, Sheffield Hallam University, October 1994.
2. P. Trivedi, 'To deny our fullness: Asian women in the making of history', *Feminist Review*, no. 17, 1984, p. 38.
3. Quoted in Liz Evans, *Women, Sex and Rock 'n' Roll*, Pandora, London, 1994, p. 235.
4. *Women, Sex and Rock'n'Roll*, p. 232.
5. P. Parmar, 'Young Asian women: a critique of the pathological approach', *Journal of National Association for Multi-Racial Education*, vol. 9, no. 1981, London, p. 74.
6. Vaisakhi is a Sikh festival, celebrating when Guru Govind Singh baptised the first Sikh, and when they were first told how a Sikh should behave, and about the 5Ks.
7. K. Burton and S. Awan, *Rough Guide to World Music*, Routledge, London, p. 232.
8. KKKings, *Mikah K*.

i was a teenage country fan

ELECTRIC
Clark
C
COMMANDOS
Brunswick
Brunswick
Juniors Club
"Make someone happy"
The Buzby Club

i was a teenage country fan

a tale of two soundtracks

rosa ainley

Decamped from Muswell Hillbilly land, north London (round the corner from the Kinks), I found myself in Diss, Norfolk, at the age of nine – another planet. The six years I spent in the metropolis of south Norfolk (the sort of place where they drank Vimto – a kind of flat coke for flatlands) made me, musically speaking, and established the habits (some good, some execrable) of a lifetime.

I lived with two older brothers, substitute parents who fancied themselves on the cutting edge of musical appreciation. And who just fancied themselves. They also had control over the means of musical reproduction (such as they were – we didn't begin to scale the heights of stereophonic technology until much later), or at least power of veto over me playing *White Horses*. That was my first single, and their sneering reaction should have warned me about what was on the way. Shuttling across the musical chasm between what they thought I should be listening to and what I listened to at school, I ended up with twin secret lives.

What I heard at home was the Grateful Dead, The Band, Velvet Underground; moving into John Lee Hooker, Robert Johnson, Aretha, Wilson Pickett, Jimmy Cliff, Desmond Dekker, lots of Trojan. Set against this there was the Fab 208 world of school. I knew quickly where the cool was, and equally quickly that setting yourself apart, at home or school, is inadvisable without allies. Anyway, being cool and fourteen is antithetical. I wanted to be listening to the charts with an earplug from my trannie and squeaking on the phone about my latest find in Snob. Adaptation between the two worlds became a social necessity.

But this necessity did not mean I liked much of what I heard through the earplug. When I look through a few titles I get an inkling of why: *Sugar Candy Kisses*, *Sugar Baby Love*, *Sweet Talkin' Guy*. I'm not pretending I really knew what the Velvet Underground or The Band were on about, but there was something there that I wanted to know more about. It was similar to how I felt, at about the same time, reading DH Lawrence and Anais Nin. You know it's dirty and you pretend you're grown up enough to understand it, and if nothing else it gives space to your imagination.

Occasionally, a hit from one life could be an advantage in the other. I was bought *Sticky Fingers* for my birthday one year and turned up at school with it. It was much admired by the older girls. (Or was that more to do with the older brother who bought it for me?) But it was sneered at by my contemporaries, who tended more towards TOTP compilations, if they had albums at all. So I could hardly ever play anything on the class record player.

Bobby Womack's *Lookin' for a Love*, and *Roots* by Curtis Mayfield were the first two albums that really did it for me. Looking at *Roots* today, I notice Curtis's up-to-the-minute longer-length suede jacket with big lapels and cool boots, as now seen at Red or Dead and similar emporia. The clothes were a big pull even then – I didn't want to look like The Sweet. I did an English project in my second year at school based on *Underground*, a track on *Roots*. I think I must have read *Brave New World* then too: it was a sort of cod futuristic, post-nuclear thing, infused with extremely vague ideas about blackness and peace and racial harmony, as it might have been termed then. (Although Muswell Hill was hardly the acme of multicultural life, Norfolk was notable in my eyes for its lack of black people. There were also no traffic lights. It was a desert, I tell you.)

Listening to soul pushed me towards other sounds I heard in their material. There's the Womack country album, for a start, on which Bobby's dad wipes the floor with him with the sublime *Tarnished Rings*. A note to recording artists: work with children if you must, but never get your parents to sing on your records – they always show you up.

I wasn't prone to analytical thought at fourteen, so I heard the connections rather than theorizing about them. Think country soul, think blues, think rock, think of work by Ray Charles, Aretha, Dobie Grey, Al Green.

But in my memory it was *Nashville Skyline* that really started the country thang. I distinctly remember one brother, who'd come back from university full of alien habits (musical and culinary), hopping around in what had been the parental bedroom in Diss to *Nashville Skyline Rag*. My reaction of 'Oh god, the brother's at it again' changed into 'Oh Yes Indeed' by about the third hearing. And Johnny Cash sings on that album too, on *Girl from the North Country*. I wasn't sure that either he or Dylan could sing, but it didn't matter, my fourteen-year-old heart was away.

Nashville Skyline Rag made me want to move in the same way soul did, and it hit me in the chest. This was a distinct and welcome contrast to the hippy music, which you could only sway to in a wiped-out fashion or whirl around to like a crazed drug fiend. Or worse, sit still to, too stoned to move, as I remember happening at a Stomu Yamashta gig to which my brothers took me, at UEA.

Piled up on our record player were singles like *Don't it Make my Brown Eyes Blue*, *The Most Beautiful Girl in the World*, and *People Get Ready*, which most people would have considered naff in all sorts of ways, least of all musically. *One Piece at a Time* by Johnny Cash was another overplayed album. I didn't know about any of the Johnny Cash 'Man in Black' stance then – later on it became a useful defence against country's political failings (until I firmed up my confidence that politics isn't the point, and is never one of music's strong points).

The Most Beautiful Girl in the World is, on one level, shlocky in the extreme, but I quickly got over that, as well as the problems it posed to my incipient feminism. In any case, the unbearably saccharine sound of my school-friends' chart music – Gilbert O'Sullivan, David Cassidy, the Osmonds, etc. – meant I had developed the high nausea tolerance associated with adolescent taste. But the power and (dare I say it) sincerity of Charlie Rich's delivery could overcome any misgivings.

As if it were Diss, Nevada, rather than Diss, Norfolk, we expanded our playlist to include Doug Kershaw, Doug Sahm, and the likes of Gram Parsons and Creedence Clearwater Revival. (The last three formed a bridge *à la* Byrds between hippy rock and country, in their different ways.) Gram Parsons reassured me that country was not all so straight: there were bad boys too. (Bad girls came much later, eagerly anticipated.) So we added the sounds of hillbilly, bluegrass, Tex-mex/west coast psychedelia to the more mainstream country sounds to which we had already surrendered.

I saw Doug Kershaw at Dingwalls, about 1976, and still thought, while I was rapt in pleasure, 'What am I doing here, listening to this strange man playing a fiddle in an emerald green velvet suit? I should be at the Roxy.'

When Charlie Rich was wowing the charts with *The Most Beautiful Girl*, my friends made it only too clear they hated it, preferring to cry over Nilsson and Terry Jacks. I kept quiet because school was another life, one of tank-tops, discos and witless heterosexual teen behaviour. I had a pair of yellow jersey flares that I wore with a black Brutus shirt and a yellow tank top, and someone dared to tell me I looked like a banana.

On one memorable occasion a friend and I went to a disco 'up Norwich', got picked up, didn't like them, went together to the Ladies in time-honoured fashion and didn't return. Eventually we re-emerged and got picked up again. Later, teenagely pissed, we tried to hitch the twenty-five miles home. No luck (or maybe very lucky indeed) no lift. We staggered to the outskirts of town and slept in a field in our high-waister and polyester finery, to be woken not by the tweeting of little birds, but by a farmer firing a gun across the field. We didn't hang around long enough to find out if he was pointing in our direction.

My parents were not around to discover these exploits, so it was not their authority that made me attempt (unsuccessfully on that occasion) to secrete them. It was big brother credibility rating. Going to a disco was bad enough, hitching without older, male company was definitely not approved of. At school, though, these were wild and daring exploits, and were exploited, ad nauseam.

The brothers also asserted their authority around my dress sense. I had this tank top, shades of burgundy (a colour that no longer seems to exist) and white, striped and ribbed, a perfect item. One day, I was wearing it under a coat of shorthaired velvet with an extremely loud pattern, somewhere between paisley and psychedelic. One of my brothers pointed out sharply that the coat (which I never liked but wish I had now) was 'easily the nicest thing you've got on'. So there.

Sometimes the two lives met. I would have schoolfriends to stay and we would hit the nitespots of Diss, which involved discos in pubs, martinis, and blowjobs. I had to try to wear clothes that looked suitable for both arenas. What would I wear? Or would they be too stoned to notice? With a friend in tow, I think I became a schoolgirl again in my brothers' eyes, and hence susceptible to all sorts of uncool behaviour. Once I bumped into one of my brothers and some of his friends in Norwich. Norwich for me meant shoplifting on my own or shopping for tacky clothes in Snob and Chelsea Girl, hanging out in that lovely mezzanine cafe in Woolworths, and snogging at the bus station. To my brother, Norwich was a place to score (drugs, records, books . . .), and visit the burgeoning freak scene, at the other end of town. The fact that I was incorrectly dressed for this meeting far outweighed considerations like not having seen him for several weeks. I felt found out and could not get away quickly enough.

Crossover, when it did happen, was very much one way traffic. One Christmas my brother bought me a pair of brown satin espadrilles, rope wedges with leg laces (to be tied round the ankle, *never* up the leg) which were very much this year's model. Like buying me *Sticky Fingers*, it was partly the equivalent of buying someone a book so you could then borrow it back, and partly a case of making me in their own image, or at least their girlfriends' image. They were unwearable to school, and languished in the bottom of my dirty washing bag.

And so it was with music. Stevie Wonder finally made it at school with *Inner Visions*, which at home was seen as comparatively low grade and – that dread word – 'commercial'. By this time I had the first in a long line of music buddies, a soulboy who knew about *Talking Book* and other essentials including *Blues and Soul*, when my classmates were getting excited about Sparks and reading *Jackie* and *Mirabelle*. When I bought *Songs in the Key of Life* with a record token it was in great demand at school, while no one wanted me to play it at home. It all left me with that anxious mix of superiority and feeling left out, which thankfully (unlike spots) is a specifically teenage preserve.

Even where there was simultaneous appreciation, it tended to be unsatisfactory. We sneered at home to the Carpenters, like everyone else, only to have to re-evaluate them a few years later when Bobby Womack covered *We've Only Just Begun*, and their sound was suddenly more to 'our' taste. Eventually even bands like Mud, whom I had already seen a couple of times (once in Swaffham Town Hall, no less), were seen as having a certain appeal. But this was on the kitsch 'n' crap scale, unlike a friend at school who told me one day that she did actually really like the Osmonds, when silly pretentious moi, with a precocious grasp of the ironic, had assumed it was all a joke.

The people at school who smoked dope were transparently sham hippies, and to be avoided. I had enough of the genuine article at home. One of the school hippies I remember was called Ginnie and played awful folky songs by Ralph McTell and Leonard Cohen on her guitar. She was rumoured to be a lesbian too, although I think this was because she was too smart (despite being musically disadvantaged) to go out with any of the dorky boys available.

A few years later, when I'd escaped school for groovy further education college in London, a girl from Bromley (a circumstance akin to trying to be a hippie at boarding school in Norfolk) said to me, during a discussion about the choices we'd made on our UCCA forms, 'But are there freaks there?'

I soon discovered the joys of *Jolene*, *Misty Blue* and *King of the Road* on pub jukeboxes, the everyday trials of love and toil. I no longer had to tap that foot surreptitiously or pretend some other jerk had put them on. At university one of my performance pieces was singing *Stand By Your Man*, gazing lovingly into the eyes of my best friend.

It took me a long time to realize that peer group and fraternal pressure in both musical and sartorial departments made me queasy, and compliance never made me feel part of the gang, just an eternal imposter. One brother has never stopped feeling able to say things to me like, 'I really don't know about the leather jacket', and 'So what are you going as?' But the way he looks now makes it impossible to make the comeback that leaps to my lips – it would be cruel.

Secrecy and disapproval were familiar to me by the time I was of adult years. When I was coming out in the early 1980s, country music was far less acceptable even than it had been at school, and now people's prejudices were clothed in politics. Not to mention all that boys' music that I listened to. In solidly Tory Norfolk we had not been politico schoolgirls; and this was before popular culture – which allows people to do degrees about quiz shows – had been invented. Football was still a game of two halves and country music was for jerks. Along with many other desperate dykes – surely they can't all have really liked Cris Williamson? – I indulged my outlawed tastes in private, and proudly displayed my double-sided Dolly Parton pinup to an intimate circle of friends.

It isn't the same any more, although, as outlaw posturing goes, being a country fan lasted a long time. Hardly anyone now calls it country and western, unless they're trying to be irritating. Everybody knows Garth Brooks sells more records than anyone; everybody expects me to like kd. What can you do? I blame the brothers.

TOTALLY
GIRL
POWERED
MARCH 1993

TOTALLY
GIRL
POWERED
MARCH 1993
velocity girls

10 velocity girls

indie, new lads, old values

laura lee davies

When I was making my first explorations into music, the decision to be an indie girl (as opposed to a metal head, a soul girl or a hippy) was guided by a few simple factors. Firstly, the tunes seemed, mostly, far more listenable than other music. Secondly, the look: what vague style it had was affordable and flexible. I don't know how much leather jackets cost, but a second-hand skirt and an M&S jumper (Altered Images chic, I guess, if it had to have a name) must be cheaper. And I sure as hell didn't want to see myself in a disco-bound boob-tube or a Donnington-bound pair of spandex trousers.

Then there were the songs themselves. It was 1981 and The Farmer's Boys, The Higsons and Serious Drinking were stumbling out of Norwich singing songs about Sergeant Bilko and being hungover. The content of their love songs appealed to a self-conscious schoolgirl, whose scraps of self-esteem went down the pan if someone so much as waved the front cover of *Cosmopolitan* in her face. These songs weren't peopled by hairy old rock stars and their lovely lay-deez. They were tales of falling in love with skinhead girls, who were into football and The Monochrome Set.

Like every genre of music, indie has its good and bad points. For every band with a real sense of humour, there have been a bunch of po-faced Kevin Rowlandses. Indie has hardly been the enduring voice of women and music, and – especially post-acid – it has fallen for some damn-fool fashions. But by the very nature of any music based on a need or preference for economy, it has had to have aspirations beyond fame and fortune, and consequently court individuality and afford the space for originality. Therefore it can be moulded into almost anything.

So, in a music unsteeped in thirty-year-old rock history and clichéd tradition, it should have been easy to push the boys around just as much as they have pushed us, and to participate in some of those well-loved indie rituals. But I only spotted for the first time a dress (a rather billowing floral print) taking a stage dive, in 1991 (The Family Cat, the Venue in London's New Cross).

For me, just like everyone else, it was actually less a matter of ideals and more a case of fitting into a gang mentality; and, on a superficial level, the artists (if not the indie media) had a softer gang mentality than the bikers, the mods, and those sad tossers who walked around in wedge haircuts.

It is not modesty but sheer embarrassment which prevents me from confessing the first couple of gigs I attended, but they were major, mainstream affairs at big, sit-down venues. It wasn't until I went to the Lyceum (four bands for the price of two on a Sunday night), and the Venue in Victoria, that I was well and truly away from the cattle-market mentality of the discos and nightclubs that, er, more self-confident teens were going to.

The more casual the door arrangement, the more welcoming the atmosphere, to the point where everyone has to make friends if they're passing each other down the tiny, damp corridor from the bar to the music room at the Falcon in Camden. It's not that the black-clad moodies who hover over the cash box are going to greet you with a tray of vegetarian snacks (unless you happen to go to the Sausage Machine on New Year's Eve), but it was easier to watch what was going on without being watched. It was easier to be yourself. Standing in tiny rooms with sparse professional lighting set-up makes a gal feel she can melt into the crowd. In fact, if you recall the early days of The Smiths, you'll remember that they used to throw flowers to everyone in the crowd, regardless of sex.

However, The Smiths are a perfect example of how indie music has always belonged to the boys. The debate about Morrissey's sexuality is irrelevant (with tales of how he was raised by his mother and a house full of females, and of his choirboy voice). With his wimp geekiness compensated for – at least to his schoolboy admirers – by an intellectual swagger (a walking Oscar Wilde quote machine), Morrissey was the hero for a generation of seventeen- and eighteen-year-olds. They could blame their continued virginity on a suddenly fashionable 'gentility' and had Johnny Marr's achingly beautiful, jangling guitar music as a sound-track to their NME-reading, fanzine-writing lives. While the chaps hitched themselves up on to the chaises longues and sang every line of *How Soon is Now?* with sullen personal resonance, we just got on with appreciating the songwriting genius, and thanking Christ that we weren't going out with anyone who makes such a meal of not having 'a stitch to wear'.

And, of course, it gave the journalists a good chance to attend to their own little-boy-lost tendencies. The seeds of mainstream success for the likes of The Smiths – who continued to be indie, if not in record label, at least in cardigan-wearing spirit – was the beginning of the end for the broader musical coverage of the likes of the *New Musical Express*. Whereas they had previously included more dance, soul and rock music in their pages, they found that they could retain most of their solid readership whilst narrowing their sights.

The final blow came with the dispute over editorial control in 1987, when the likes of Stuart Cosgrove departed, taking with them any support for a more open-minded paper which had also written about television and politics as well as a wider range of music. The success of comedy has seen the eventual return of television coverage, while film and dance music are covered as a necessity, but the paper's musical direction has, for the main part, never looked back, taking upon itself the role of indie music's principal voice.

The success of magazines such as the *Face* (specifically into dance-based music) and Q (aimed at the grown-up CD rock market) has given the NME another reason to abandon wider musical styles.

A keenness to sell papers by giving the readers 'what they want' has resulted in year upon year of new indie names thrown on to the cover like so much shit against a wall, and those who stuck (Happy Mondays, Stone Roses, Carter The Unstoppable Sex Machine and Suede) have found themselves grinning from the newspaper racks four or five times a year. In narrowing their range, the NME and *Melody Maker* have retained some importance in indie circles at least – bigger fish in a smaller pond. It is for this reason that the writers behind them are still relevant, but despite the promising rise in the number of female journalists at both papers, they are still run on a boys'-club mentality. Neither of these publications (nor *Sounds*, which was first on many of the American indie scenes that shaped British guitar music in the last decade, before its demise in 1990) needs to be guided by the sexist rules of corporate business. Their immediate big-brother worries come from their IPC owners' blanket rules about using certain bad language and their lack of respect for unions. But they are still edited by males, writing mostly about males, and writing for males. In such an environment, it is not surprising that many of us have to admit to occasionally thinking of a female artist's success as some great achievement, and not something which is perfectly deserving and natural.

I went to a girls' school and, whilst having several friends who listened to indie programmes like John Peel and Richard Skinner, it was not until I found males of a similar age that I found anyone who was regularly prepared to go to gigs, get involved with fanzines and run a club. If we no longer have to sit in towers and get on with embroidery, combing each other's hair and dying of 'being a girl' by the time we're nineteen, most of us know women who are just not interested in taking as active a part in music as our male counterparts. So for most of indie music's history, it has been easy to pander to male tastes, with the voices of female journalists like Jane Suck and Julie Burchill as the exceptions which allowed the rule.

When Ngaire-Ruth, a female *Melody Maker* journalist, was the first person to go back to her paper raving about this tight, female-led trio called PJ Harvey she'd seen in a Hampstead basement, she was eventually granted (weeks late) a tiny amount of column space in the gig reviews section. When the boys consequently trundled down to check the band out, *Melody Maker* were quick to claim this new discovery, even running their first major PJ Harvey feature with a copy of an earlier gig review, presumably to show how on the case they were. But it had originally been printed long after Ngaire's first wise words.

Ironically, Polly Jean Harvey has been championed as the outspoken voice of women in music: in her sheer ability to write songs with a thunderous tone; in direct, explicit lyrics; and, most scarily of all for those boys in the front row, in the way she looks them in the eye.

The press, typically, has turned this self-confidence into a rare, marketable commodity. It is seen as almost frightening, rather than empowering. On days when Harvey decides to smile, put on make-up or more recently a dress, the tone has usually been one of victory, 'the taming of the rock chick', rather than simply seeing this as another side to another artist's personality.

A Q magazine cover (May, 1994) featured PJ Harvey, Björk and Tori Amos with the cover line 'Hips. Lips. Tits. Power.' Was it not the case that they had found three females to lump together to make a 'women in rock' issue, rather than having to feature each artist separately? Perhaps I'll forgive them the day they put Mick Jagger, Paul McCartney and that bloke from The Spin Doctors on the cover, arm in arm, with the cover line 'Hey look: three people with penises making hit records!'

There does not need to be a malicious misogynistic campaign on the part of editors and their contributors. I'm sure that *Melody Maker* in the late 1980s, when its covers were being dominated by women – Throwing Muses' Kristen Hersh and 10,000 Maniacs' Natalie Merchant, for example – never thought they were being sexist. They were probably proud of their appreciation of these female-led bands and the likes of Hersh are certainly capable of looking after themselves. But the rarefied language and approach of the paper's journalists at the time only served to make these women into indie music's own 'special ladies'. No one can question the sincere enthusiasm for the music of writers like Chris Roberts, but by early 1989 when Lush were feeling queasy at the sickly journalistic poetry of his review of one of their earliest gigs at the Cricketers in south London, his commendable reputation for breaking female-fronted bands was becoming one of the business's running jokes.

Despite the seemingly feminine, or certainly less macho nature of so much of indie music's lyrical content, almost all of the genre's leading 'scenes' have, over the years, been quite male-dominated, if not laddish. At the time of the C-86 boom – which took its name from an NME tape featuring the leading bands of the 'shambling' scene in 1986 – the anorak was king. Bands like Primal Scream were fusing post-Jesus And Mary Chain feedback with fey vocals. Others, like The Wedding Present, were taking their queue from bands like The Smiths; their words were more domestic and openly vulnerable than the swaggering self-confidence of rock. However, no matter how harmlessly wimpy the likes of Lawrence from Felt or Stephen of The Pastels seemed, they still belonged to a movement made up entirely of blokes. The Soup Dragons, The Bodines and Mighty Lemon Drops – not only does it read like a list of major label signing failures, but there isn't a female band among them.

Even so there was enormous value in the musical influence of the C-86 scene (if in a delayed reaction, after acid house lost its way); and in the way it revitalized the power of the indie label. The opulence of the mid 1980s had allowed major record companies to hoover up any budding talent, leaving the indies without their financially beneficial leading lights. At least its do-it-yourself sound and philosophy, the return to a Smiths-like purity, meant that going to gigs and reading (or writing) music features about non-macho boys was a less alienating experience again.

The same goes for the 'shoegazers' who shuffled along at the beginning of the 1990s. The epitome of loud guitars and shy-boy presence, the likes of Ride and Chapterhouse were making stunning music and adding the sweetness of schoolboy voices. The few who have survived the scene have developed as more mature rock artists. Their boyish moments are now more in line with the naive charm of something more cred (like the Beach Boys in their darker moments) than with the inexperienced tone of boys whose mums might still pick them up from Oxford station if they've been up to town for the day.

In February 1992 I interviewed Thousand Yard Stare. They were pleasant enough, and our meeting was certainly made easier by the fact that I could match them drink for drink. Between the lines of their banter (there were five of them), it seemed to transpire that only two of them were particularly well-versed in sexual practices. One of these had a regular girlfriend, and the other, a bit older than the rest (who were still of tender years, and not concerned so much with point-scoring as simply picking up a few tips) seemed to have got around a bit. The band made the usual laddish jokes and seemed to be taken by some kind of trend of using Vick's vapour rub to enhance their, erm, chemical pleasures. But, when moving to discuss uses for other items readily available in the medicine cabinet I happened to refer to another's advantages during anal sex, they all seemed to go rather quiet. Ah well, you can't always be one of the boys.

But, despite the mesmerizing voice of Rachel Goswell, who guested on Chapterhouse's classic *Pearl*, there was still scant female presence in the movement. A radio producer and A&R man said to me that if someone came along with the same sound but a female voice, they'd clean up. The wise words and strikingly elegant tones of The Sundays' Harriet Wheeler had already made her a goddess amongst the music press. In an interview in *Time Out* (7–14 February, 1993), the band's bassist, Paul Brindley, pointed out: 'The rumour that's been going round the media that Harriet is an angel from heaven is not, in fact, true.' But they were not particularly part of any tangible scene. They were, luckily for them, purely a talented band in the tradition of fine guitar-based indie music.

Lush, whose songwriting and guitar-playing power fell to the band's two females, Miki Berenyi and Emma Anderson, were not afraid to mix hard, fast guitar sounds with unashamedly high-pitched, typically girlish vocals and harmonies. But interviews were openly self-confident confessions about sex, drinking, and all manner of not typically feminine subject matter. They were, as ever, patronized by a few journalists and adoring male punters, but a mouthful of Miki Berenyi's personal politics has always been enough to shut the troublemakers up.

And then there was Curve, who blended the crystalline feedback of the more subtle 'shoegazing' sounds with thunderous pop hooks and Toni Halliday's purring, cooing, growling vocal performances. Both she and music-maker Dean Garcia were older and wiser than their indie contemporaries and, for both their albums, managed to sidestep dependence on Toni's appeal as a cherry-lipped gothic-haired angel.

The streams of journalistic poetry for Cocteau Twins' Liz Fraser flowed on, but at least the arrival of her first child (with fellow Twin, Robin

Guthrie), just before the release of their *Heaven Or Las Vegas* album, seemed to put off any ideas that Fraser could be anyone else's girlfriend purely by some process of listening to the band's records.

And then of course there were the other, more aggressive male-dominated indie scenes, like the indie-dance explosion of the late 1980s, which centred around Manchester's 'Mancadelic' sound. Blending the heavy beats of acid-house, an indie guitar scene, the drawling lyrical cockiness of a drug-fuelled generation of brash young things, and a street fashion which was cheap and non-designer-led (though you could always find a baggy, washed-out sweatshirt with the right label at an over-inflated price), indie-dance was indie in label (mostly), media interest and guitar techniques alone. The likes of The Stone Roses, Happy Mondays and Inspiral Carpets were healthily supported by the NME, and press shot after press shot of spotty white males would have you think that the indie spirit was not dead; but it was the laddish, sexual leeriness of dance music which spouted forth from Shaun Ryder's lips.

Happy Mondays did have their moments of pure genius. Their female singers were busty, brassy (and black) sex symbols who, whilst making the array of lads on stage look rather like a sad bunch of stag-nighters on their way home, were more fitting in the traditions of funk than of indie. The band should therefore have become part of something completely different. But the Happy Mondays' demeanour owed more to the conventional rock mainstream tradition, and they could not have been more divorced from the polite, sometimes idealistic, middle-class views of their listeners.

However, the images and ideas being thrown out by these bands influenced the rest of indie music greatly, a genre more prone than most to the effects of an imperial new wardrobe. (Someone quoted me an NME journalist's answer-machine message, which at one tragically misinformed point announced proudly that if the caller wasn't ringing about 'The New Wave Of New Wave' then they might as well not bother speaking after the tone.) At the time of indie-dance, it was impossible to make it through the first bar of a song without a wah-wah pedal cracking into action. The more excessive and 'don't care' the sentiments and videos that went with these songs, the better.

The fact that Happy Mondays achieved the peak of their celebrity status when Shaun Ryder and Bez spent a day editing *Penthouse* magazine and got to be soaped-up by a bevvy of beauties in the bathtub afterwards, pretty much sums up why being a female music journalist became a rather unappealing duty for a while. The success of bands like Oasis is reminiscent of these earlier bands not only in their meteoric rise to importance and their energetic guitar-powered sounds, but also in their media-friendly reputation for being working-class lads who enjoy a spot of rock 'n' roll hotel trashing. Such behaviour will always be part of a genre of music which largely appeals to the studenty crowd looking for the thrill of what they don't know, combined with the low-fi domesticity of what is utterly familiar to them.

When NME took it upon themselves to pronounce Happy Mondays as beery lads with dodgy politics, towards the end of their glittering career, were the rest of us supposed to look quizzically at our copies of *Pills And Thrills And Belly Laughs*, and the forests of newspaper that every publication had devoted to the wild and wacky ways of these blokes, and be stunned into a new realization? It was only the arrival of fresh blood, in the shape of new musical trends, which prompted a more distanced view from the 'monster' they had perhaps not made, but certainly reared.

While Britain was gripped by this new acidic disco fever, places like Boston and Seattle were flying the flag for America's unerring belief in guitar bands. Whilst our own post-dance raves included Ride, James and Carter USM, Boston was producing bands like The Pixies and Throwing Muses. They took their cue from Sonic Youth's notion that not all hard US rock had to emanate from Californian boulevards full of babes, or rerun average-America's full-throttle doom-rock tradition. Rather, it could be harnessed for more tuneful purposes and to hammer home a more dry, articulate and witty (in the broadest sense of the word) music. Although many of these slacker-rock anti-heroes, like Dinosaur Jr, were half-indie/half-'rawk' band (in music and spirit), and still boys only, both The Pixies and Throwing Muses had a strong female presence.

Half-sisters Tanya Donnelly and Kristen Hersh shared the vocal and songwriting responsibilities in Throwing Muses, and Kim Deal was just as strong a voice of The Pixies as mainman Black Francis. The influence of Donnelly in her own (chart) successful band Belly, and of Deal with her sister, Kelley, bassist Josephine Wiggs and (male) drummer Jim MacPherson in her present band, The Breeders, has been assured, confident and effectively eloquent. Neither has particularly been painted into the corner of female-artist labelling. As you'd expect, there have been those waiting in the shadows with paint-pots at the ready. But the wry humour with which, say, The Breeders posed (girlies waving from the back of an open-topped car with Jim at the steering wheel) for their *The Last Splash* album, has brushed all such nonsense aside. Live, their brazen strengths have not once detracted from their femaleness.

Despite being an articulate figure, Hersh has had her moments of inconsistency; the topless photo session for one of the weeklies was a typical example of how she sometimes finds herself playing someone else's game. When I first met her in 1988, the success of artists like Debbie Gibson and Tiffany was mostly what the achievement of females in pop had to offer. 'I find that really offensive', she said. 'Because sixteen-year-old girls have always been the most fascinating people I've ever met. They're right in between, they have the intuition of women and the intuition of children, the naturalness of children and the desires of women. They're in between worlds, being fascinated by both, and there's no reason why they should be saying those dippy things!'

A taste for the hard and fast nurtured the popularity of British bands like Teenage Fanclub and House Of Love here, but it wasn't until the emergence of female hardcore bands, like Babes In Toyland and Hole from America, that the evolution of 1990s indie rock was given a more solid female voice. Grunge, superficially one of the most alienating musical styles, was simultaneously developing, but from within it an increasingly successful female hardcore had enough following to grow into something autonomous.

In America, the popularity of eloquent, outspoken female singers like Courtney Love, the sheer power in the growl of Kat Bjelland from Babes In Toyland, and the rise of a strong female teen spirit in the country's magazines, saw the beginnings of what was dubbed Riot Grrrl. Over there, this was a more sophisticated and humorous statement, which tackled female issues with assured poise, whilst letting loose a few sonic devils and alleviating a simple punky rage via the likes of cartoon rebel gal Tankgirl.

In their travels, British music paper journalists like Everett True hooked up with bands like Hole, and returned to England with news of girls who were having more than their share of fun. Fellow *Melody Maker* writer Sally Margaret Joy also picked up the theme, and the paper became the focus of Britain's own Riot Grrrl scene. But by the time the ICA took the movement on board for a day seminar in 1993, the paper was among the first to dismiss the whole shebang as a lot of grrrls with little to get excited about.

Bands like Huggy Bear, who were half-male, half-female, were a mix of eloquent rhetoric and positive actions. Their singles, like *Her Jazz*, preached power to females via a 'boy-girl revolution', without the 'die male whores!' message that often gets dragged out at the same time. Their anti-press stance, whilst being somewhat self-righteous and self-consciously rebellious, at least served to make their voices heard louder on the occasions when they did grant a journo an audience. And the irony of their female-only gigs, when the band was half-male itself, wasn't lost. Theirs was simply another powerful, loud indie music, but this time the women had the first and the last say. Labelmates Bikini Kill, however, choose not to dilute their message, despite also including a (token) male in their number. The lyric in their song *White Boy* sums up their rather unforgiving sentiments: 'White boy . . . don't laugh, don't cry, just die!'

The attention paid to other (mostly or all) female bands like Mambo Taxi and Voodoo Queens, by everyone from the music weeklies to *Mojo* – the epitome of old cronie muso-ism – also gave women a break. More interested in singing songs about chocolate, dreamy Keanu Reeves, and telling crap blokes to get stuffed, for male writers the appeal of these bands was in the fact that they weren't well-mannered little girls. Articulate Voodoos lead singer, Anjali Bhatia, was quick to put down tokenist interest, replacing curiosity with an awareness not only of the female voice of indie pop – be it campaigning or purely having a good laugh – but also issues of racism and female power throughout the music business. Their single *Supermodel Superficial* was a success in both male and female quarters.

As Riot Grrrl has become a lost phrase – along with 'shoegazing', 'lurching' and all manner of other fleetingly all-important press tags – so the New Wave Of New Wave took its grip. Thankfully, the prominence of lead singers like Elastica's Justine Frischmann (originally elevated to celebrity status because she was someone's ex-girlfriend: Suede's Brett Anderson), and Echobelly's Sonya Aurora Madan, has largely been down to the content and abilities of their bands' songs. That said, certain male music journalists have sneered at Sonya's enthusiasm to 'mouth-off' about serious issues such as abortion and anorexia in her interviews, whilst wholly empathizing with Manic Street Preachers when they have been talking about the same issues. However, with tight-fit t-shirts reading 'Big Boots, No Knickers', the likes of Elastica have made their sheer cheek as brash as their New Wave-inspired music, appealing to lusty young boys and girls of all sexual persuasions.

I see more women at gigs now, which is great. Perhaps the world of indie is a more equal place, or perhaps this is a product of post-feminist tenaciousness. It would be a shame to miss out on The Sundays' beautiful, intelligent guitar music live, just because you can't stomach the cries from the first five rows for Harriet Wheeler to get her tits out. There will always exist the likes of PJ Harvey's producer Steve Albini, who called his Big Black follow-up band Rapeman, not out of maliciousness but because of some comic-reading college-boy sense of humour. And music magazines have mutated to the point where *Loaded* is just as likely as anything else to be on Blur's interview itinerary, with the piece printed between pages of limp porn and sports reports.

There is nothing to be gained in ignoring all these things, but the increasing female presence at gigs, in the press, and in bands, adds a voice to a predominantly white and otherwise male musical culture. At least now we don't just have the faded black and whites of The Raincoats to look back on, and we might not find ourselves mourning for the 'good old days' any more.

Q
A
Z

the joy of hacking
Litton
IMPERIAL

11 the joy of hacking

women rock critics

caroline sullivan

Given that rock criticism is about the easiest branch of journalism to break into, because of the need for large numbers of free-lances to cover dozens of records and concerts each week, it has always surprised me that more girls don't try it. Despite there being more women journalists than ever before, we are still outnumbered by – using the *Melody Maker* staff box as my statistic – around three to one. On the national papers, where only two or three people are employed by each title to cover rock, there are almost no women. At the time of writing, I'm the only female principal rock writer on any of the broadsheets, and one of only two on the rest.

So what gives? There are much worse career choices than pop criticism. It's interesting, and mildly glamorous, although it doesn't feel that way when you're plodding home in the pre-dawn chill after reviewing your fifth concert in as many nights. It can be reasonably lucrative, and you get to vent your spleen, in print, about all manner of pop-related topics.

The perks are well-known: free records and concert tickets, the chance to meet your favourite stars – who usually turn out to be irredeemably short and married – and foreign trips, although the recession has pretty much curtailed those. And you get to listen to music all day. But most critics are male, not to mention white and middle-classish. Many have degrees, but are willing or able to work for the music press's miniscule freelance rates because it seems like a cool job. And there's always the chance of graduating to one of the nationals, or to a TV presentership.

So why don't more girls do this, then? The reasons, I'd venture, are these: it can be intimidating approaching music mags, most of whose pages reek of male bonding and footie references. Secondly, there is a drastic difference in the way men and women use music. Men get banal about it, filing CDs alphabetically, scrutinizing lyric sheets for hours, and treating the outpourings of a pet band as deeply consequential.

Maybe this is because of the same inherent gender difference that makes them enjoy taking things apart to see how they work. Or maybe it's because music gives them an opportunity to combine the male love of gadgetry (expensive stereo systems) with the desire to express themselves (the latter often found difficult by teenage boys). Interestingly, but maybe not surprisingly, dance music – that cosmos of computers and electronic gizmos – is made almost exclusively by men.

At the risk of generalizing, women are more sensual and instinctive about things. And most women are able to revel in music without needing to analyse it. We lack the trainspotter gene that makes men want to write about a particular guitar solo as if it were the Sermon on the Mount. Here's an illustration of same from a 1994 album review by a guy:

> On *Slide Away*, a gorgeous rock ballad, Oasis approach the – sorry about this – ragged glory of Neil Young's Crazy Horse. *Definitely Maybe* is the exact point where pop meets rock. Noel and Bonehead (guitarists) duel like bastards all over the place for space in the mix.

Much music journalism consists of exactly that – attempting to describe the indescribable with adjectival gems such as 'her crystalline piano playing' or 'his whingy yet resonant voice'. (I should know – those are mine.)

The relative dearth of women is a shame, because this is one of the only male-dominated fields where being female is a positive advantage. I kid you not. Publicly at least, pop music sees itself as a left-wing art form. Most of the industry has more or less liberal politics, even though it exists within a capitalist context, and sexism is officially unfashionable. It exists, but not overtly. So when an editor discovers a woman who can write, he – and it's usually still a he – tends to give her work. It may only be for the kudos of having a real live girl on the team, but so what? For every editor who hires a woman tokenistically, another takes her on for her ability. We're in a position of strength. They know we're under-represented, and they want to, or need to be seen to, redress the balance. Even if I'd been hired solely to present the 'women's view', I wouldn't care. I've never allowed myself to be marginalized. I've got a big mouth, and tend to blurt out what I think.

If confronted with an equally talented man or woman, editors will, in my experience, opt for the women. The problem then is finding women who want to do it. My own entry into music writing was fairly typical. There's no degree in pop journalism (yet anyway) – you have to improvise your way in. I was working as a message taker – my official title – at a computer company in 1984, when a friend showed me a review she'd had published in an American pop mag. I was impressed and wildly jealous, because I'*d* always wanted to be a rock journalist. How dare she?

Thus goaded, I decided to do something about it. I blagged an interview with the then up-and-coming Smiths by saying I'd been commissioned by a Los Angeles magazine. To my surprise, the ruse worked. I duly interviewed the guitarist, Johnny Marr, went home and wrote it up in what I imagined was music-paper style, and sent it to half a dozen magazines. I was shocked when an American one wrote, saying they liked the piece, would use it, and wondered if I'd consider being their 'London correspondent'.

For the next year, I wrote a fortnightly column, for which – I could hardly believe it – they paid me. I received about £70 for each 3000-word piece, which seemed like a fortune to me. In 1985, I began eight years of freelancing for the *Melody Maker*. I had myself a time. Five years and thousands of album reviews later, *Melody Maker*'s ex-features editor, who had become the *Guardian*'s pop writer, invited me to do freelance gig reviews, and things went on from there.

When I became the *Guardian* main pop crit. in March 1993, I was petrified by the responsibility. The paper had never had a woman in the job and I felt compelled to excel. I somehow felt that the fortunes of all female rock hacks depended on my making a success of it – probably not an unusual feeling for women entering any field where they feel under-represented. When I finally settled into the routine, I found myself really enjoying it. I think my boss, the paper's arts editor, hoped for a different – i.e. female – touch in a field swamped by men.

I am able to say that I've never encountered sexism in the *Guardian*. Any nonsense I've experienced has been directed not at me as a woman but as a rock critic, and that's because a few of the other *Guardian* critics tend to regard pop as something of a lesser art. 'Who's *Morrissey*?' one of them daintily sneered at a meeting. (Thinking about it, who *is* Morrissey? Describing him as he is, an eccentric Northerner who raves about vegetarianism, didn't exactly support my case that pop should be taken seriously.)

The most stressful part of the job is keeping up with what's going on in the notoriously fickle world of pop; a seemingly endless whirlwind of short-lived trends and fashions. In making what have to be largely intuitive decisions about what to cover, I have made mistakes. My most embarrassing ones happened at the *Melody Maker*, where I convinced the editor that the future of rock'n'roll were a couple of groups called Boys Wonder and the Ghastly Girls and wrote long pieces to that effect. But the thrill when I choose correctly is considerable.

The *Guardian*'s readership is mainly educated and left-of-centre, and I take this into account when deciding what to write about. It's not necessary to be quite so on the cutting edge as in the music press, but I do have to monitor trends and be adaptable. For instance, when ragga became popular in the spring of 1993, I had to write a piece on it with three hours' notice. Knowing nothing about the subject, I frantically called some people who did, and managed to put together a piece that sounded reasonably informed, though I have to confess to hoping that my readers would know even less than I did.

One of the best things about being in a position of some influence is being able to spotlight female bands, especially alternative ones. I choose the records I review each Friday, and it's delicious to be able to feature people like Courtney Love and Scrawl alongside your Eltons and Erics.

Another positive aspect, although it's taken a while to accept it, is the realization that, as a critic for a major paper, I *do* have influence. It was brought home to me a while ago, when a friend told me that a workmate, who didn't know me, had bought a copy of the Rolling Stones album on the strength of my favourable review. Both startled and rather thrilled with myself, I told a female editor about it. 'Women have trouble feeling confident', she replied. 'I had trouble even calling myself a journalist for a long time because I thought it sounded too presumptuous; but I've known guys who've had, like, one review published somewhere, and *they* think they're journalists.'

When I began my present job, my increased status got me a lot of attention from press officers. They're the tenacious souls whose task it is to convince hacks to write about their artists. PR, being a 'service' profession, is dominated by women, one or two of whom are known to flirt with male journalists to get their bands covered. (Oddly, no male publicist has ever done this with me – too afraid, maybe, that I'll send a squad of incensed girls to beat them up for their impertinence.)

Curiously, I have run across sexism from just one press officer. A major label's female head of press, known for her matey relationships with male writers, has never invited me to lunch or offered me any exclusive interviews with her groups. Okay I'm whinging, and everybody should have my problems, but it is irritating. Lunches are the tribal drums of the music biz, and not to be asked is a snub. When one of her artists released a new album a couple of years ago, she took one of her male critic friends to St

Petersburg for five days to interview the guy. I was lucky to get an audience with him in the record company's London office, sandwiches not included.

People often assume that bands make sexual advances to me. ('Come on, they must – you're a girl, and you're around all these guys ... ') Fortunately, or unfortunately, they don't. In ten years of doing this, only two men of the hundreds I've interviewed have so much as favoured me with a rakish smile, and even they seemed happy to leave it at that. I don't know whether or not to be insulted.

Oh, but I'm forgetting the fellow from Right Said Fred. Not one of the bald ones, but the third guy. I rang him in Tokyo for an interview, during the course of which I mentioned that I had broken my knee and it was in a cast. Whereupon he mused that he'd never had sex with anyone in a cast, and wouldn't mind trying it when he returned to London. I wish I'd come up with some snappy put-down, but I couldn't think of one. So I laughed in a 'what a jolly jape' sort of way. It must have put him off, because I never heard from him again, thank God.

Apparently critics used to get propositioned regularly, but times have changed. Even the most Neanderthal of rock stars seem to have absorbed the fact that a woman journalist doesn't necessarily equal babe-trying-to-get-acquainted-with-musician's-undertrousers. Even if one were tempted, the quick hotel room tussle that would result wouldn't be worth the damage to one's reputation, the double standard being alive and well. Take these two dreary stories for example.

A chap of my acquaintance, a fellow hack, was wildly notorious for bedding some of the women he interviewed. How he persuaded them I can't imagine. Eventually he acquired thrush, or something like it, from one of his conquests. When word got around, people – and not just men – found his story interesting and entertaining. I believe some of his more blokish friends went 'Fwoargh!'

Contrast that to the reaction received by a woman writer who slept with a lumbering Celtic guitarist. Her colleagues were disdainful, and her editor was annoyed that she'd behaved 'unprofessionally'.

Apart from that, what are the negative points to being a woman in this industry? The main one is that you find yourself treating male co-workers in a hail-fellow-well-met fashion. You don't become a lad exactly, but you adopt a protective saloon-bar amiability. It comes of hanging round with guys in the office and while out doing interviews or reviewing gigs. Perhaps that explains why male and female hacks don't often get romantically involved with each other.

Another difficulty is the unsocial hours, and having to go to shows alone. This problem isn't unique to women writers, but I believe it's more significant for us. It isn't reviewing gigs on my own that I dislike – that happens to us all as friends tire of the novelty of going to concerts for free. It's all the late-night travel. London being huge, with relatively few venues, you're guaranteed to live miles from wherever the gig. The further away, the more certain it is that the band will play an extra-long show which makes you miss the last tube. There's nothing more dismal than waiting for a night-bus in Wembley on a freezing winter night (the only sort of night anyone ever seems to play there).

The positive side of this is that you become very self-reliant. There will never be anything enjoyable about riding buses in the small hours. (Yes, you can take taxis and claim them as expenses, but sometimes you don't have the £20 to spare.) But handling these situations makes you more assertive.

Earlier I mentioned that music-paper readers tend to be male. As well as aforementioned factors like men's obsession with the minutiae of music, there's also the propensity of the newsprint to transfer itself to the reader's hands. Reading *Melody Maker* or the *New Musical Express* is literally a dirty job. Readers of the *Guardian*'s music pages also seem to be predominantly male, but not as disproportionately so. The letters I receive are mostly from men, and are almost invariably complaints about negative pieces I've written on their favourite bands (my favourite said simply 'SLAG!'). What post I do receive from girls is usually positive and encouraging (although one misanthrope and pedant in Birmingham once wrote, 'Diana Ross's first concert here was on Friday, not Saturday. What do they pay you for?'). It also tends to be women producers who ask me to do occasional pieces on the radio.

I'm entirely biased – I prefer interviewing women. The task of gaining someone's trust – or, at least, grudging co-operation – when you've only just met them and are going to ask them questions about their personal life, seems easier when you're the same sex. It's amazing how bonding it is to have periods. You can approach the interview as a conversation rather than an interrogation, and the results can be most fruitful. One rather austere lady singer, warmed by the glow of our forty-five-minute acquaintanceship, confided that she'd once broken wind in a church confessional booth. As she memorably put it, 'I let out a little ripper.' Another discussed the tribulations of being celibate when the rest of her band were in relationships.

Reviewing albums and concerts by women is also more fun; again it's the spirit of comradeship, however spurious that may be. Because of the obstacles most of them have had to surmount, women artists are more interesting. The ones who've reached the top and stayed there are twice as bright and manipulative as men, and that fascinates me.

But women can be just as obnoxious as men, natch. One summarily ended an interview because your reporter didn't know the name of her new single. Then there was the female rap trio who conducted an interview sitting on me – two on my legs, one amidships – because they thought it was a great wheeze. They split up some months later. Ha! Generally though, women are better, more obliging interviewees, possibly because, like the rest of girlkind, they were raised to try to please.

But I sometimes find myself tolerating artistic mediocrity in women when I wouldn't in a man. I've never written an unjustified favourable review, but occasionally I'll find reasons to excuse an uninspired performance. Last year I reviewed a West End musical version of the life of the country singer Patsy Cline, boringly titled *Patsy Cline – A Musical Tribute*. The singing was all right – damned good, in fact – but the acting was grim. You should have heard the British cast's attempt at Nashville accents. But they were all trying so hard, and their plight aroused my sympathy. I began seeing things from their perspective, which is lethal for a critic. Okay, they're terrible actors, I reasoned, but American accents are hard to do. And they're really good singers, and they've got such nice costumes. I ended up writing a moderately negative piece, instead of the complete pasting I'd originally intended. (To my astonishment, some of the other reviewers actually liked the thing.)

I probably shouldn't pull punches. Boy critics never seem to have any qualms about delivering good, sinus-clearing slag-offs. On the other hand, I don't have trouble criticizing women if I feel at odds with them politically or aesthetically. I'm not especially ambivalent about it. Every so often, however, I'm assailed by a pang of conscience, and revive my ongoing internal debate about what critics are for. Is anyone entitled to criticize another's work, and what gives *me* the right to pass judgement? This may be linked to my inability to play an instrument, and faint admiration for anyone who can.

What riles me more than anything is women stars who allow the men around them to run their careers. I'm sick of the phrase 'We women have to take control of our lives', because it has become anodyne, a cliché. Of course we do, and we all know it. Having said that, it's surprising how many successful women don't mind ceding authority to male managers or record company execs. Janet Jackson's 1986 album, *Control*, was supposedly her declaration of independence, but she simultaneously confessed in an interview that her favourite way of cutting loose was to throw grapes out of the window, especially if she was in a tall building. Is this a girl who manages her own career?

I also took exception to Samantha Fox, who had her father sit in on our conversation. He was apparently there to make sure I didn't give her too hard a time. Please! She was bearing her bosom on page three, yet dad didn't trust her to deal with a hack. This was an example of how sharing the menstrual experience sometimes doesn't bond you in the slightest – I bristled at the sight of her, and she at me.

Notwithstanding, the days of marketing pop singers as bimbettes have, for the most part, passed. Those showbizzy, tits'n'bums outfits like Hot Gossip and Toto Ceolo don't seem to exist now. As I write, I'm looking at the cover of Toto Ceolo's only hit, *I Eat Cannibals*. The Ceolos are posing in what appear to be bin liners that have been torn to show cleavage, and they are wearing strappy little stilettos. Even their names – Lindsey, Lacey and Anita – sound archaic, like the kind of girls who hung around at Stringfellow's in the 1970s. It's impossible to imagine a record like this being released now, except as a kitsch joke. Even Kylie Minogue writes some of her own songs, and chooses her own producers nowadays, whereas male groups like Let Loose are the closest things to the airheaded and airbrushed babes of a decade ago. Perhaps it's the novelty of men acting like simpering fools that makes it so enjoyable to review them.

So progress is being made. I like to think that, in my way, I'm encouraging girls to do their own thing. Rock journalism isn't a bad job. You should try it – and if we meet, I'll give you the phone number of the guy from Right Said Fred.

HARVEY GOLDSMITH ENTERTAINMENTS

ACCESS ALL AREAS

ARTIST

DATE 11/6

VENUE

access some areas

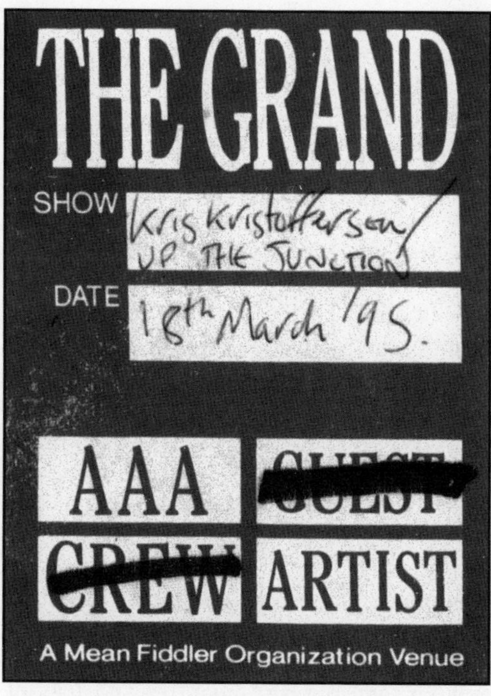

12 access some areas

pr in the music industry

sarah cooper

Public relations, publicity, press representation, promotion, it goes under a variety of names but is usually abbreviated to PR. A very twentieth-century phenomenon, when art can no longer speak for itself, PR can become the lens through which the image is filtered to its audience or market. This is the power of the impression rather than the actual, as the shadows cast by the artifical light of the MTV video become the reality – often even for the artist themselves, as they too become convinced that the shadow is them.

Despite its name, public relations rarely deals directly with the public. That is the constituency of its near relative, advertising. Rather, PR focuses on the decision makers, the taste makers; those who determine what the public will receive through an ever multiplying choice of media: TV (terrestrial or otherwise), radio, the printed word.

Everyone could have an image, anything can be promoted or represented; people, products, organizations, events and PR can do it for you. Once associated solely with the entertainment world, PR has become an essential item not just for rock singers, but also charities and Labour politicians. Even countries use PR. When Kuwait was invaded by Iraq, they employed a PR company to help convince the USA to go to war on their behalf.

PR's own image is somewhat sensationalized. It has a notorious history and an association with dirty tricks: the 'gossip' columns of Hollywood, the stage management of the private lives of such stars as Rock Hudson. Talented though Elvis Presley was, what set him apart from his probably equally endowed contemporaries was the ruthless vision of his manager and manipulator, Colonel Tom Parker. More recently PR has become associated in many people's minds with the excesses of the 1980s, when figures such as Lynne Franks, Magenta Divine, Bernard Ingham and Tim

Bell became as well known as the people or products they were representing. (More so in some cases – who can remember Sigue Sigue Sputnick?)

If the rise of PR has contributed to a world where style dominates over content, in such a world music is no longer just music; it is sold as a lifestyle accessory, an epitome of cool, an indicator of taste. Or those associations are used to sell something else, the ubiquitous backdrop for selling other products, e.g. cars, jeans, building societies.

Inevitably, given the number of records that flood the market each week, it isn't just raw talent that makes a hit. Something else must make it stand apart, and that something is usually the result of a well-managed and imaginative PR campaign. If a dictionary offers a definition of PR as 'the art or business of promoting good will', in the case of music, promoting notoriety is probably just as effective, as Malcolm McLaren would testify. But while PR devices play a part in shaping public tastes and perceptions, it is a two-way traffic, as the best strategies must also respond to the *Zeitgeist*. As well as embodying fantasy, music has always prided itself on its authenticity. If the 1980s gave us stars such as Madonna and Prince, who were the very embodiment of artifice, creatures beyond the preoccupations of everyday life, the 1990s have made stars of Kurt Cobain, Garth Brooks and kd lang – concerned, vulnerable and rather more mortal. Even in black music, where the powerful legacy of artists like James Brown ensures that a sense of theatre persists, current stars such as R Kelly still obviously cultivate the street in their dress and body language. In fact every attempt is made to make stars seem more, rather than less, like us – just more fortunate.

Even if music embodies romance and dreams, the day-to-day reality is more mundane, even in the field of image making. It is just another business, another arm of the multinational-dominated 'leisure' industry. Even the word 'indie' now describes a spirit or attitude rather than the ownership of the labels, who are more often than not bankrolled by large labels, and act as feeders for the mainstream. And like any other industry, it remains essentially a boys' club, with the accompanying values and attitudes that suggests. Nevertheless, women have carved out niches for themselves in the music industry, and PR is one of those. Given the hyperbole that inevitably surrounds PR, it seemed easier to get a more accurate idea of what goes on on a daily basis by actually letting two women, Liz Naylor and Regine Moylett, talk about their work and experiences.

It is very easy to draw crude analogies about the role of women: the caring for (mostly male) artists, the massaging of egos, the courting of (often male) journalists and DJs. Yes, there are certainly women who will fall into those stereotypes, and Liz talks about 'the twittery end of PR'. But Liz and Regine, both self-aware and assertive women, are far from that.

If people think what goes on in PR resembles an episode of *Absolutely Fabulous*, both Regine and Liz show that the reality is more prosaic. The day-to-day existence is more run-of-the-mill than might be popularly supposed, mostly spent with the phone clamped to your ear, trying to persuade journalists with jaded palates that this is the record they really should play, or the gig they really should be at.

This is an occupation without a clear career structure, and both Regine and Liz hit on their jobs in a more or less accidental way. If for some music PRs it could as easily be washing powder as Take That, many of those involved genuinely love music, as do Regine and Liz. For them an emotional connection is there, even if it can be whittled away through day-to-day familiarity, and the grim predictability of the fate of most of their charges.

Between them, they have been involved with a broad range of popular music, from the internationally-known artists such as U2 and Van Morrison, whom Regine represents, to the indie world in which Liz is immersed. But it is here in these grimy rooms that scenes like Riot Grrrl and Queer Core are played out, which can have broader repercussions on the future face of music.

Liz Naylor

I'd left home and got involved in a fanzine in Manchester for a few years. That led on to managing people and promoting gigs, if not altogether successfully. I moved down to London and worked for an indie magazine called the *Catalogue*, compiling listings, hardly exciting stuff. But the editor set up an independent promotion company, which she asked me to join, and this was, I suppose, my first entry in the music business proper. This was the early 1980s when there weren't many independent promotional companies around. Things were still very naive; literally all you would do is just send off records to music papers and more often than not they would just get reviewed.

I can't believe it now, I worked in an incredibly naive way, I was just thrilled to get free records. I was seriously underpaid, but to me it was just such a buzz to be involved with something that had been part of my life since I was eleven years old. I don't think I was very self aware at that time, I was just into taking as many drugs as I could and going to gigs, and that's, in a way, how everybody starts. There will always be a constant stream of people who work in the music industry because they want to do that.

It's very different now. I don't think music has changed particularly, but publicity does seem to have got very bland and safe, revolving around fewer and fewer bands. Companies have less money to spend, and people working in it treat it more like a job. They don't go to gigs all the time, they go into the office at nine and leave at six. And the tools have changed: you have word processors, you can knock out press releases and biographies really quickly. In my day it was banging it out on a typewriter, I can remember not even having a fax. Now, if you're late with a press release – just fax it through. Want to get hold of a journalist – just send a fax. Maybe this offers a better quality product. Certainly people are much more professional, none of this hanging around in the bar with journalists and then missing the band you'd brought them to see, which happened to me.

I only started realizing how being a woman affected my existence in the industry about five years ago, quite late on. In the early 1980s, I had fled from the women's scene in Manchester, which I found insufferably right-on and leg-warmerish. It was the time of Greenham, and I felt very alienated from all that, but because I was a lesbian it was more disappointing to me. But I was just a furious punk rocker who was hell-bent on taking as much speed as I could possibly get up my nose. So my awareness of my role as a woman in the music industry was not exactly foremost in my mind.

But it gradually becomes something you can't put your finger on; it's an unnamed source of grief in your life which, I only recently realized, becomes too unbearable if you acknowledge it. I don't want to know. Yes, the music industry is like any other industry, like the car industry or whatever . . . it's ultimately a cynical machine. But most of the people involved in it are totally besotted by music and you get very emotionally involved in the job, so the last thing you want to know is how shitty and sexist it is.

It's hard to say how women relate to music without going into the bounds of 'gosh we're more sensitive'. The music industry is very coded and very impenetrable to most women. Rock music takes some investigation, it can be very alienating for women. But they probably listen to music in a normal way without feeling the need to absorb all the mindless detail. Anyway, a knowledge of music is not something a woman displays in public, like peacock feathers. When I was at One Little Indian [an independent record label] I probably knew more about music than anyone else in the office – like, I could do the Q quiz – but it was always assumed if you're a girl you don't. If you listen to boy journalists talking about music, it's always a competition, like, have you heard so and so – it's all point scoring.

So, as a way of coping with it, you become one of them, more often than not; an honorary lad. That's certainly the way I coped with it. You can almost find yourself despising women because they don't know anything about music, and that's a terrible trap to fall into. But for most women, how they find out about music is through blokes: either boyfriends, brothers, people at college.

There are a lot of women in the industry, but they are mostly in very dull jobs like production. The high-ups in the big distribution companies are usually men, whilst the girls are involved in production and in moving thousands and thousands of records from one warehouse to another – not very exciting jobs but these are precise and complex jobs where a lot can go wrong.

There is of course another role. There are loads of women in PR everywhere, not just in the music industry, the assumption being that pretty girls will get you or your product somewhere. Why else are there so many female radio pluggers? Radio is hell anyway. The BBC is weird, it's another set of codes. Like some debutante's ball, you have to almost curtsey to the right people. It's a really specialized area and incredibly highly paid. But it's a horrible job, the person delivering that record to the radio station has got to have thirty-six-inch legs. EMI or whatever has all these bimbos who are just couriers, while the copy is written by the heavyweight boys running the department.

That's the twittery end of PR, but all those women are hard as nails of course, they have to be. In that context I was pretty much a freak, and so you have to trade on that, you're the one who can go drinking with the lads. But it's all a bit of a battle. It's a bit tiresome to have to deal with people on a false level all the time. Ultimately I wanted to move over to marketing, but it was impossible – it was like, you're in PR, that's your job because you're a woman. Why are there so many male journalists, why do girls wear pink and boys wear blue?

As for being a lesbian, no one really talked about it, but I'm sure I was badmouthed behind my back. Once I had to go to America with a female journalist and the joke going round the office was that it was because I wanted to shag her. It was horrible, and the woman herself found it deeply offensive. But she was pretty cool about the whole thing, and we went and had a good time. I think that record companies are kind of scared of sexuality, and they were scared of me, although I don't think I realized it at the time. But as for gay men – well, from the 1950s, the pop end of things at least, has been dominated by gay men.

For some unknown reason – and it's certainly a mistake I made – you feel the music you're promoting is for the greater good, and here to enlighten and improve the world. But really it's just like anything else, it's there to make money and eventually just as tedious. After a while you just know how it will go for bands unless they're exceptionally smart, and you might come across someone like that once a year, like your Suede or whatever. Ninety-nine per cent of bands are doomed to failure: their aspirations are just too fettered by the white male rock world they are part of. Maybe women have got better things to do. There's a lot of sitting around and going to your mates' houses involved in being in bands – desperately dull. They've usually led fairly limited lives; left school, joined a band, got signed, did a tour in a van, and that's their life, and it's reflected in the songs.

But women artists are different, even if they 'left school, joined band' kind of thing, I think their inner lives are perhaps a little more developed, plus it's a more interesting story just for them to get to be in a band. Whereas it almost seems like any boy can do it and pick a guitar, play it not very well and find themselves with a page in the NME. That said, this current thing about having girls in bands will probably pass over, and next it could be about having a disabled person in your band. Well, probably not on that quite level but probably not far off it. Or more likely it will be to do with dance and black culture. There's been a hint of it this year what with Fun-Da-Mental and Echobelly, perhaps Asians will be the new tokens.

After I left One Little Indian, I lived in Portugal for a while. When I came back, I read a couple of articles on Huggy Bear and Bikini Kill. I'd had six months away to brood on it and they seemed to articulate my reasons for leaving the business. I realized that every three years, it's pretty obvious why, I leave the music industry in disgust. So I started my own label, Catcall, to put stuff out by Huggy Bear and Bikini Kill.

I think now that the pieces written about Riot Grrrl were actually more important than the people involved in it. They were just taken as ciphers by writers, often women, who saw Riot Grrrl and thought, yes, this is me they are talking about, and wrote it up. The older women got it more than the 'kids' who were just being a bit bratty and short-sighted. And, if I'm brutally honest with myself, when it failed to deliver I just thought, fuck, it was all rubbish. It did get very coy and girlie. I thought the whole idea was to build a Terminator sort of woman musician, but it turned into girls in skirts playing recorders, insufferably twee.

It's still happening in America. Just because of the size of the country, things are reported more slowly, so there is more time to grow. Whereas English music often never has that time to develop, which can throw up lots of interesting things, but it can also mean it doesn't go anywhere. If Riot Grrrl had another year to ferment, I think it would have been much more potent. It would have attracted more people who had known what they were doing, and drawn in more feminists, though I can't imagine *Trouble and Strife* readers going mad for punk rock. But some of the early plans were to go into schools. That sounds really corny, but if, when I'd been a kid, they'd come to my school, I'd have gone, 'Yeah, I'm going to form a band now!' You know there's enough right-thinking teachers in place, but it never carried through those initial ideas because it all blew up so quickly.

Riot Grrrl criticized the tools of the industry which very few bands do, though they might whinge on about it. But they said, 'we hate the press', and got a front cover out of it. Whereas punk was against everything else really . . . the establishment, the Queen, etc., and it was taken up very quickly by the music press, who loved it. But Riot Grrrl was one of the first things to be actually against the music press, which it saw as the devil, though it's obviously more complex than that. It was all a bit naive, but in a way it was absolutely right. Fuck Madonna going on about being punished, those kids were very punished by the press for standing up and saying this is all sexist bollocks. But thank god someone actually said it, even if it was really confused thinking. That was always an argument levelled against Riot Grrrl by the music press: that it wasn't clear, it had no clear aims. But name me a band that is . . . rock and roll is about confusion, teenage confusion. I mean what are the clear aims of a band like Oasis?

I went on to get involved with Sister George and the Queer Core stuff. Queer Core started off as a sort of joke in the wake of Riot Grrrl, and it has steadily gained momentum. Now they don't even care about the music press, they don't even read it. It's a reaction to the 'gay community'. They're working-class kids and they feel incredibly alienated by the Old Compton Street scene, and the new improved version of being gay, all that shopping and cappuccino. They're angry that it's all about being groovy, like the Wow Bar being on Mariella Frostrup's show. Whatever happens next, it was really nice to see two pages with the word queer all over the *New Musical Express*. It's totally unique post-Stonewall; there's a bunch of gay people who know about music who are getting involved in it. And it should inspire more lesbians to form bands at least.

PR is like any job you go into because you were passionate about it. It changes the way you view things or listen to things, and it's hard to stay a fan. Just like if you talked to a lighting engineer, they'll probably say they spend all their time at a gig watching the lighting pattern. Mystique is crucial to music. But once you've worked in it, especially indie music, it tends to lose it. It's actually one of the least glamorous jobs I can think of – standing in a grubby room and listening to a not very good band. Even if they are any good, you can almost plot their course, a page in the NME and then, in a year's time, chip paper. Now I like music that's far removed from my experience, like American music, which still has a lot of romance for me. But, like a lot of American literature, it's probably about a world that doesn't exist. But it certainly existed in my teenage imagination, and I'm still plundering it.

I think music is probably more hypocritical than other industries, because music is meant to be about being cool, it's not about calling women birds, and black people . . . well, you know. But it won't tackle any of those issues head on, in fact it feels above it. And that's my ultimate criticism, it's really smug and fails to address anything.

Regine Moylett

I used to be a musician; I started to play the piano when I was about eight and I played the piano and the violin until I was about sixteen. I was in the school orchestra and the school choir. The school I went to was very musical. We went in for lots of competitions, which we won; I really liked that. But by the time I left school what I wanted to do was be a currency dealer – I thought I might be the first woman currency dealer in Ireland. There was actually a women currency dealer in Belfast at the time and I went and worked with her for about six weeks, which was great. But then punk happened and everything went a bit wonky. I joined a band as a keyboard player, and we made one single and two tracks on a couple of compilations, and we did loads of gigs – we played about three hundred gigs in three years. But I realized that it wasn't for me when we did a residency in a sort of punk café in Tralee, and this Swedish tourist, a backpacker or something, stood in front of me for the three nights we played at this place, mouthing 'I love you, I love you'. It completely did my head in and I thought . . . I don't want to be famous.

But I also thought I didn't have the outstanding talent, although it's drive as much as talent that keeps people performing – but I felt I didn't have that either. My older brother was in a band who were very popular at that time, the Boomtown Rats. He and I went out Christmas shopping in Dublin and he just had an awful time. Dublin is really cosy, and people would just come up and say, 'I think you're brilliant', and attach themselves to him for the rest of the after[noon], or be abusive to him. We went for a drink at about six o'clock, and this guy came up to him and said, 'Buy me a drink, you millionaire', and Johnny said 'OK'. And then he went, 'You can't buy me with your drinks', and stumbled off out the door again. I thought it was horrible. I'm sure it meant nothing to him at the time and that it would roll off me now. But it really did affect me back then.

Though I had always wanted to do something to do with music, getting involved in PR happened because one thing led to another, not through any conscious decision on my part. The music industry in Ireland in the early 1980s wasn't very developed, so that was one of the reasons I came to live in London in 1982. I didn't know how long I would be here, but I just stayed – it's often the way. I did various odd jobs, most of them music-business related.

I worked for a music-business lawyer, in a little label out in Wembley, did some writing for the NME for eight months or so, and in doing that I came across Rob Partridge of Island Records. He offered me a job as a junior in the press office, which I took because I thought I could do with a wage for a while. I ended up staying there for eight years, and then I left in 1990 and set up my own company. I did take some of my Island artists with me, such as U2, Marianne Faithful and Gavin Friday, which the company were fine about it. I'd known U2 in Dublin but we didn't get on particularly well then. I wasn't a rock fan, I was in a power pop band, but after a few years at Island I did became their publicist.

The term PR makes me uncomfortable; to me that's more about product, marketing and a general public awareness. But what we did at Island, and what I do now, is simply press representation. I think Island has a good attitude towards its artists and to publicity in general. There were never any publicity scams, or any of the other things that seem to happen elsewhere, going on. I do know there are elements of PR that aren't straightforward, and I would never want to do anything grimy, or shocking, like the things done by the old school. If you read the Frank Sinatra biography, they purposely bussed people in to create a scene, so the press would cover it. I remember this guy coming into Island and telling me he had a gig where balloons fell from the ceiling at the end of the gig, and there was a pound inside every balloon, and the press went wild, and so they got really good reviews. I thought ... oh really. I don't find scams remotely interesting. But you do come across people who set them up all the time.

In the same way, I've come across artists who are addicted to publicity and have to have something reported in the paper or they think it didn't happen. They don't see the difference in it being reported in, say, the *Sun*, that they were at a party, and someone in a quality paper saying this record is quite good. Apart from the genuinely talented, there are a lot of nasty characters involved in music, and publicity is what makes them into nicer people. If the papers show them smiling and enjoying a joke at some launch, then that persuades them that they are nice.

When I first started at Island, Frankie Goes to Hollywood had just been signed, and it was great. I was put in charge of them and they went through the ceiling, and we ended up getting a press award in the first year. When *Relax* first came out, it did OK, went in at number seventy, then to thirty-five after a few weeks. When Christmas came, a new American remix came in which was much better, and I remember the Head of Sales worked over the holiday making sure these remixes got into the shops. Then Mike Reed said on the radio 'ooh this is dreadful' and banned it.

The following promotion meeting was very tense, it wasn't going be on TV or radio any more, it all had to be down to press, there was no other outlet. Derek Chinnery, then the Controller of Radio One, had said I'm not interested in playing records about 'sexual deviation'. Mary Harron wrote a really interesting piece in the *Guardian* using that quote, and pointing out that the record is really about ejaculation, and wasn't it interesting that the controller of Radio One considers ejaculation a deviation, my goodness, isn't the country full of sexual deviants! That was a turning point in the story, apart from being a good record, it became a controversial and newsworthy one. When Derek Chinnery retired years later, he said with a chuckle that he wanted more time to Relax.

Once it was banned, the record shot up the charts to number one and stayed at the top of the charts for about twelve weeks. Meanwhile, the 'three lads' were providing great copy for the tabloids all the time, and of course, as Holly and Paul were gay, from every aspect there was something to write about. And then came those slogan T-shirts. There were a lot of people involved and they all came together and the results were remarkable.

Though people think press is women's work, I don't think that there is any work that is either men's or women's, and I think it's insulting to ghettoize tasks in that way. Actually the entire music industry is run by women. In every department there are far more women, particularly in the workings of it: warehouses, packaging, manufacture, the creative side – design of sleeves, etc. I don't know if it's on a par with other industries or whether it's better or worse, but hopefully women are now getting better positions. Certainly in my early days at Island, when I first took over the press office and had to attend high level meetings within the company, I was the only women there, and they were obviously not used to having to put up with women there that much. I used to get so annoyed, I turned into a complete flag-waver; the slightest comment about a female artist used to get me on the soapbox, and it wasn't really a useful communication skill at all. But gradually there were more women appointed and that made it easier.

But I don't think the music industry is any better or worse than the world at coping with women. I know that there are people in the industry who think women shouldn't have children and work, and some of them are quite powerful, but I've not seen them impress that on anyone. I know that's not to say it's not going on, and I do think there is victimization and prejudice. But I think it's the result of particular individuals, rather than a policy or a conspiracy. I have worked for men, one man in particular, who hated women and drove me (but also everyone else) demented.

Being Irish in the music industry is not too bad. There are a lot of Irish people in the music industry, and in the media too; probably the biggest ethnic group. The industry in Ireland is not big enough to employ many people, yet the number of artists from there is proportionately huge. The average record company office in Ireland is quite small, and to have a big hit you only have to sell about 12,000 records. That's not enough to support a big staff, and I think that's why a lot of people move from there to here. But also Ireland is a very family orientated community, and if you don't feel like fitting into that, you leave.

I feel relatively comfortable with being Irish in England, but I do get a bit tired of it sometimes, because some people still use the word Irish as an adjective to mean less than intelligent. Even someone like Clive Anderson does it – not that I'm holding him up at as some paragon of virtue, but you'd think he'd be relatively well informed.

I don't wake up every morning thinking I'm going to put things right but it's very irritating on an everyday level. I remember when we'd got new computers in the office, and I was sitting there trying to fit a piece of text on to a particular size of paper, and the two guys I was working with were standing behind me thinking it was hilariously funny, going 'What's this, paddy logic?' But I just got on with it and it worked.

Now that sort of thing is really irritating, but I'm not sure you can do anything about it, and it has got easier over time. Certainly, moving out of that and working on my own, I can avoid the insidiousness of it all. But it may easily be there, and I may still hear about it, but I don't feel it. I don't feel downtrodden in any way, but I feel very lucky as I don't think my experience is necessarily typical. Too many women are not encouraged to take charge of their lives, or can't, and that's a terrible resource wasted.

I actually employ all women at the moment, but it's a happy accident and I have employed men on a short-term basis. Usually what we do is get someone in for a short period of time when it's busy. If they are really good, we like them, and a position comes up, we keep them on; but we're so tiny that we can't take many people on. At Island when I was responsible for hiring and firing, there was about a fifty:fifty mix. I've worked with some very good men, and some jerks, and likewise some good and awful women. But I have to say it is really nice working with all women – when you drop something on the floor, you don't have to bend down in a vertical drop like a Bunny girl!

I do find it harder to be critical about women artists. I feel that I would want to go that little bit extra to be supportive of women and Irish people, or any clan that I belong to. I think it's quite easy to pick holes in people, and women especially, and the things that can irritate are sometimes to do with femaleness. But certainly women are better communicators. That seems to be fundamental, and that can help a lot.

I could probably do press work for most 'things', but I don't think I'd find it that interesting. We don't represent objects or products or concepts, like Coke or Radio One, but performers, and I'm more interested in people. And it would be the same if they were actors or writers. I feel PR is about the public's perception of something, but we're more like a mouthpiece to the press. We deal with the media who then write about it if they feel moved in some way. I don't think that many people really think about the process of making records and how hits actually happen. In fact it probably isn't that interesting or important to the music fan. Just like people don't think about how cars are made.

It's basically all about information and communication. I like that, I like being able to go and talk to the person who has chosen to create something, and then try and find somebody in the media who can understand what that's about . . . that's what fascinates me.

I can still get disappointed sometimes when a journalist is just too busy to cover a record that I really like, or because they think no one's heard of them. But I like journalists to have strong opinions. There should be more of them, to put more personality into a piece. A lot of pieces are just factual accounts, rather than people going out on a limb for a record just because they like it.

I can carry on this work as long as I find the people I represent sufficiently interesting. I need to like them, or at least think they have something to say, or think what they're doing is good in its area. Otherwise, how can you ring a journalist and say with some sincerity, please spend an hour of your life listening to this record. I'm still a fan, and I like a lot of different music. I must have my choral hymns, and if ever I got a place of my own, I would have to get a piano so I could play it again. I like live performance, and even now I go to gigs a lot. But I still don't know what possesses people to get up and do that. Because of that little Swedish man in Tralee, I can't.

contributors' biographies

Rosa Ainley is a journalist and writer, now thankfully returned to north London. She is the author of *What Is She Like?*, a study of lesbian identities (Cassell, 1995), and editor of *Death of a Mother: Daughter Stories* (Pandora, 1994). She continues to play the same records as she did when she was fifteen, though her wardrobe is rather more contemporary.

Sairah Awan is a freelance music journalist and researcher specializing in youth culture and race. She studied Media and Communications at Sheffield Hallam University and is currently working for Boy Atlas Productions as a documentary researcher, TV researcher and Press & Publicity Co-ordinator. A vinyl freak, her pride and joy are her record collection and her 1970s Fender Mustang.

Jennifer Barnes is a writer and musician. She has given lectures for The Royal Opera House, Covent Garden, London University, and The Royal Academy of Music. In 1994 she translated Janáček's *Jenůfa* for the English National Opera. She has contributed the opening chapter, 'Television Opera: A Non-History', to *A Night in at the Opera*, published by the Arts Council of Great Britain, 1995.

Cath Carroll endured several years of teenage blight in Stockport where she was a member of the Mud Fan Club. In 1979 she met Liz Naylor and they formed the unpleasant, strongly Fall-influenced Gay Animals. She wrote for the *New Musical Express* in the mid 1980s and was later signed to Factory Records as a solo artist. She now lives and records in Chicago, Illinois.

Sarah Cooper picked up her orange plastic Beatles guitar at the age of seven and has never looked back. She is a journalist who has written for a number of publications, including *Diva*, *Shebang* and *Trouble and Strife*, as well as contributing to *The Good, the Bad and the Gorgeous* (Pandora, 1994).

Laura Lee Davies is the music editor of London arts and listings magazine *Time Out*. She is a regular contributor to Gary Crowley's indie-orientated music programme on Greater London Radio. In her countless interviews with bands, she has discussed music and politics but mostly argued about football.

Sophie Fuller is a musicologist, writer and author of *The Pandora Guide to Women Composers: Britain and the United States, 1629–present* (Pandora, 1994). Although she specializes in the lives and music of women composers in late Victorian and Edwardian Britain, her musical passions range from Hildegard of Bingen to Me'shell N'degéOcello. She also works for the organization Women In Music.

Helen Kolawole was born in London in 1969, grew up with Grandmaster Flash, Run DMC and now runs with Snoop Doggy Dogg and company. After graduating from London Guildhall University where she specialized in African-American studies, she found success as a freelance journalist. She currently works for *The Weekly Journal*, a black broadsheet, where she has written for both the arts and news desks. She looks forward to a day when she can listen to a rap track without cringing at the lyrics.

Lucy O'Brien is a writer/broadcaster and author of *She Bop: The Definitive History of Women in Rock, Pop & Soul* (Penguin, UK and USA, 1995). She has also published two biographies, *Dusty* (Sidgwick & Jackson, 1989) and the best-selling *Annie Lennox* (Sidgwick & Jackson, 1989, St Martins Press, USA, 1993). A contributor to various titles including *Vox*, the *Guardian* and *Cosmopolitan*, she began life on the *New Musical Express* and believes the future of rock'n'roll is female.

Sue Steward is the Arts Picture Editor of the *Daily Telegraph*. In her other lives she is a journalist writing mostly about music from Latin America, the Caribbean and Africa, as well as from the outer fringes of rock and soul. Alongside writing she has worked as a club DJ, radio broadcaster and TV producer of music documentaries. Her first book, *Signed, Sealed and Delivered: True Life Stories of Women in Pop* (Pluto/Serpents Tail, 1984), was co-written with Sheryl Garratt, now editor of the *Face*. It remains a unique analysis of women's input into pop history. She is currently working on a book about salsa. Sue lives in London.

After growing up in New Jersey with a fondness for pop music and writing, **Caroline Sullivan** was delighted to discover that one could make a living by combining them. Now rock critic at the *Guardian*, she has also written for the *Times*, *Melody Maker*, the *Independent on Sunday*, *Smash Hits*, *Cosmopolitan* and, to her eternal ambivalence, *Penthouse*.

Val Wilmer, who is still in love with Margie Hendrix, wrote her first articles on music while she was still at school. A prolific commentator and photographer, she was the first woman involved with the modern liberation movement to write about women in jazz, in *Melody Maker*, *Let It Rock*, *Spare Rib*, *City Limits*, *New Socialist* and *JAZZ Magazine* (Paris). Her book *As Serious As Your Life* (1977), a key source work on the 'free jazz' movement, includes analyses of women's social and participatory roles – regrettably brief, she admits, yet a pioneering departure at the time. Her autobiography, *Mama Said There'd Be Days Like These*, was published in 1989.

index